W

ILMMAKING

FILMMAKING

narrative

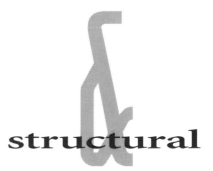

structural

techniques

BOB FOSS

SILMAN-JAMES PRESS
Los Angeles

First Silman-James Edition

10 9 8 7 6 5

Library of Congress Cataloging-in-Publication Data

ISBN: 1-879505-14-2

Illustrations: Bob Foss (film squares), Niels Hofman-Bang

Cover design by Heidi Frieder

Printed and bound in the United States of America

SILMAN-JAMES PRESS
1181 Angelo Drive
Beverly Hills, CA 90210

PREFACE

This study is not an academic treatise. It does not pretend to offer incontrovertible truths about the nature of film or television. No rigorous scientific method has been adopted when structuring the material. No systematic references are given to account for the sources used. Examples from films and TV programs are selected on a purely eclectic basis.

The material in this book is based on my own experience over the last twenty years of what works and what does not work when films or TV programs are being made. The point of departure as well as the overall aim of the study is a practical one. Two simple principles have guided the selection and the presentation of the material: 1) The terminology, when defined properly, should be accessible to any reader with a serious interest in film practice, irrespective of his or her academic background; 2) The principles put forward should be immediately applicable to his or her own work with film or TV. Any theorizing that does not meet the demands of these two criteria has been left aside.

The purpose, then, has been to find a workable theoretical framework that secures the organic marriage of theory and practice. My feeling is that film theory, when divorced from the practice of filmmaking, will lead to little more than academic speculation of minor value to the practicing filmmaker. On the other hand, film practice, which is not guided by a thorough theoretical understanding of how the medium works, may easily degenerate into mindlessness and self-indulgent sloppiness.

Many of the rules and principles arrived at here are the outcome of discussions with students at film courses and workshops. Usually, the participants of these courses have already had extensive practice in film or television. It is not uncommon, at the end of these sessions, for a student to say:" Yes, I've done many of these things more or less intuitively, but I've never been able to say why I did them." And that is the reaction I hope for. It's a matter of common sense, really, and very little else. There is no magic behind the various rules of filmmaking—just a set of principles that are the result of a hundred years of trial and error on the part of filmmakers attempting to communicate with their audience. No rules are sacred—there are absolutely no rules that cannot be broken. But you'd better know what you're doing and why. Breaking rules because they limit you is one thing; breaking rules because you have no idea of structure is something entirely different. The present study is meant as a guideline only. The reader will determine what to use and what to ignore in accordance with his or her own experience and understanding.

The material has been organized under two headings: "Narrative Techniques" and "Structural and Dramatic Techniques." There are no sharp borders between the two. The first category mainly refers to those tools and principles of film narrative that are basic to the medium, irrespective of the type of film or program one wants to discuss. The second category mainly refers to the various principles that unite the parts of the film to the whole.

A major division is made between the Dramatic and the Epic. It should be noted that the term "epic" is used here in the European, not the American, sense of the word. The more or less Brechtian, European tradition emphasizes principles of program construction that are generally ignored in the American literature on the subject.

When discussing the Dramatic and the Epic, I have—somewhat arbitrarily—divided each category into "elements" and "structure." The reason for this is a wholly practical one. Several of the elements making up a dramatic narrative may also be used in films or programs that are predominantly epic in structure. And, in the same way, a drama may sometimes introduce epic elements. The possibilities of combination are unlimited and the reader should, I think, constantly bear this in mind.

Film scenes represented by illustrations in the text are accompanied by quotations from the dialogue. All quotations are from the finished films, not from the original screenplays.

Bob Foss, Stockholm, 1992

CONTENTS

NARRATIVE TECHNIQUES

STRUCTURAL AND DRAMATIC TECHNIQUES

NARRATIVE
TECHNIQUES

1

CONTENT AND FORM

In most cases it is futile to speak of content without form. Even in abstract art, we look for content—a meaning—in what we see. The division of any cinematographic expression into content and form should be seen, therefore, only as an analytic operation.

The designation "sports car" cannot really exist in a film as an undefined generic term; we see a particular sports car that has a particular appearance, from a particular angle, in a particular type of light, and so on. Similarly, the designations "large" and "small" cannot exist on their own; an object (e.g., a sports car) is only large or small in relation to other concrete objects of comparison (other sports cars, trucks, toy cars, etc.).

When we talk about content and form, we mean two different ways of approaching the same concrete expression as it appears, undivided and organic, on the screen. In *narrative* audiovisual media such as film and TV, content and form can be approached in terms of a Plane of Events and a Plane of Discourse.

Plane of Events and Plane of Discourse (The *What* and *How* of Film Narrative)

The *Plane of Events* is the content of a film or a TV program. By this we mean the factual or fictional world that the film or program tries to depict, including everything that is or might be found within the bounds of this factual or fictional world. Anything that belongs to the Plane of Events can or could be perceived by the characters in the film or program. When all the elements of the Plane of Events are finally in place, they constitute what is referred to as the *story* or *action* of the film.

The *Plane of Discourse* is the form of the film or program. This means all the elements of form or narrative devices that a filmmaker uses to communicate a factual or fictional story to the audience. Unlike elements on the Plane of Events, the elements on the Plane of Discourse are imperceptible to the characters in the film. The various elements of the Plane of Discourse (such as camera angle, shot composition, etc.) do *not* belong to the factual or fictional world constituted by the Plane of Events but exist outside of it and independently of it. They often act as a comment on or interpretation of what happens on the Plane of Events; they express the filmmaker's attitude toward his subject.

Let us imagine the closing scene of a feature film depicting the lives of three soldiers during World War II. In this scene, we see the three soldiers running joyfully through the streets of a small French town. They have just heard that the war is over and that their side has won. Happy townspeople mingle with them amid embraces and laughter. They pass a church and hear its victory bell ringing out over the town. This is the film's Plane of Events.

It is recounted in the following way: First the camera follows the three soldiers in a long, giddy track through the streets. At the church the soldiers disappear from view, while the camera pans past the church and stops at the deserted churchyard, which we see is full of recently placed crosses. On the soundtrack we have heard the joyous sounds of the liberated town. During the pan, however, this real sound is faded down and replaced by a string of dismal, dissonant piano chords.

The main significance of this scene (which would be one long take) is not at all apparent on the Plane of Events. Everybody was happy and gay. Yet the film ends on a sad note. This is created by panning from the happy soldiers to the deserted cemetery, together with the ominous music. It is as if the camera, in panning from soldiers to graveyard, wants to say, "We won, but was the victory worth the price?" This highly significant pan does not exist on the Plane of Events; the soldiers cannot protest and try to hold the camera back as it swings away from them. The camera does not exist within the fictional world of which they are part. The camera's behavior only exists on the Plane of Discourse as a *statement* on the part of the filmmaker about what is happening. It is a message from the filmmaker to the audience of which the characters in the film cannot be aware.

(Later we shall see some examples of how the camera can be present on the Plane of Events, e.g., in certain types of documentary and journalistic films. However, this is rare in fiction films.)

EXAMPLE: Losey's _Accident_

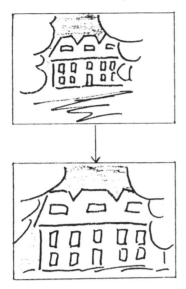

During the opening credits we have a general view of a typical English country mansion. It is dark and a light is at one of the windows. At first we hear the noise of a jet plane roaring over the house, then all is quiet again except for the bird song and the sound of a car, which for a moment we can make out in the distance. From the house comes the faint sound of someone working at a typewriter.

When the credits finish, the camera slowly begins to track in on the house and once more we hear the sound of the car, which is obviously approaching at high speed. The camera stops moving and, at the same time, we hear a violent crash followed by complete silence. A few seconds later a dog barks and a light comes on in the hall of the house. A figure appears in the doorway.

The meaning of what is communicated in this opening scene is rather _more_ than the mere Plane of Events tells us (i.e., that a car has crashed near an isolated house). The meaning is given by the way picture and sound work together. We do not _see_ the car crashing. If the film were about the people in the car, our attention would be focused on them at such a dramatic moment.

But the film is not about them; it is about the destruction of a safe and secure bourgeois way of life. The camera begins to move in on the house (the visible symbol of middle-class self-sufficiency) _at the same time_ we hear the car approaching. The camera stops _at the very moment_ we hear the crash. By means of the narrative device of tracking, a close connection has been made between the crashing car and middle-class security. The act of tracking, which exists only on the Plane of Discourse, augurs the approaching catastrophe for the people who live in the house. This is exactly what the film is going to deal with.

2

POINT OF VIEW

It goes without saying that a film or a program is narrated, that is to say it is organized, formed, and presented by someone.

Naturally, an entire team works behind the product, and a program is the result of the creative efforts of a number of people. But, in general, there is *one* person who, in the final analysis, is responsible for the final overall appearance of the product. For simplicity's sake let us call this person *the filmmaker* or *the storyteller.*

We always see a story *from a certain point of view,* and it is the filmmaker who chooses and represents this point of view. He can try to conceal his particular point of view or he can declare it openly. For example it is not uncommon for the filmmaker to try to hide his point of view, in documentaries and news reports so as to appear objective and unbiased. The material speaks for itself—"this is how it is." However, the filmmaker can also declare his position and tell the audience that he arrives at his conclusions by looking at things from a particular vantage point. This vantage point can then be considered *appropriate* (or not) in relation to the material being studied, and it is the filmmaker's responsibility to justify his choice.

One of the first things to decide before choosing a point of view is whether we want to see (or appear to see) events from the *outside* or the *inside.* Is the story told from a position inside the factual or fictional situation that is being depicted or does the filmmaker select a position outside the situation so as to have a total and commanding view of it? On the one hand we might have a journalist in a war zone, reporting what he sees and hears, and on the other, a historian who is reconstructing the history of the persecution of Jews. However, the one point of view is not necessarily more objective than the other; all we can say is that the historian's vantage point is more privileged because he is distanced from the reality he is describing (the Plane of Events) and has much more freedom to choose his material and the way of presenting it.

Where we place the storyteller has an effect on *how* we perceive the story he tells. If he is in the midst of events, we tend to accept that he cannot be all-seeing and able to answer all our questions. It is easier to acknowledge that the story is limited in its perspective and, as a result, more open to subjective judgements.

Presence or Absence of the Storyteller

The fact that the story is told by *someone* does not necessarily mean that this person is directly and openly involved in it. On the contrary, in dramatic feature films, the storyteller (usually the director) tries to conceal his presence as much as possible. What happens on the Plane of Events should speak for itself and the audience should forget that someone is pulling the strings.

The storyteller may elect to make his presence visible, however, by acting as a commentator. His voice guides, explains, summarizes, and fills in the gaps of the story. He can also appear as himself on the Plane of Events, as often happens in investigative documentary films and reports. Or he can give part of his role to one of the characters in the film, as happens when we receive guidance and comments from such a character's "internal monologue." In this case, however, the real storyteller is still present outside the Plane of Events; he still chooses the narrative style of the film as a whole.

Roughly speaking, the storyteller's position can be categorized as follows:

1) Omniscient point of view.
2) Character-related point of view (including first-person narrative).
3) Neutrally observing point of view.

OMNISCIENT POINT OF VIEW

When the filmmaker (storyteller) adopts an omniscient point of view, he stands outside the factual or fictional situation being depicted and has an overview that the characters in the film cannot have. He can be either directly present (e.g., as a commentator) or indirectly present as the invisible organizer and form-giving agent of the story.

In principle, the omniscient storyteller can relate to the Plane of Events in whatever way he chooses, with no restrictions other than those he imposes on himself. What he wants to say does not necessarily depend on documentation on the Plane of Events; indeed, his statements can *contradict* what we see there. As a narrator, he treats facts and events on the basis of insights in which the characters in the film have no part. He is always on a level higher than the segment of reality he describes.

CHARACTER-RELATED POINT OF VIEW, INCLUDING FIRST-PERSON NARRATIVE

A character-related point of view tries to limit the perspective of the story to the world as it is perceived by the characters in the story (whether the situation is factual or fictional). In other words, the storyteller attempts to see the situation as the characters in the story see it, without having access to information that the characters themselves do not have. Like the omniscient storyteller, he can be indirectly present (his presence is not seen but rather felt, as the organizing agent behind the story) or he can be directly present by giving a soundtrack commentary.

The first-person narrator is a special type of character-related storyteller. He acts as an accompanying commentator inside the head of one of the characters and we see things as this person sees or remembers them. Here the storyteller is present on the Plane of Events. The first-person narrator can be the *protagonist* (e.g., Scorsese's *Taxi Driver*), a *secondary character* (e.g., Herzog's *Aguirre*) or a more or less uninvolved *witness*. A reporter present at the events he is describing is a special kind of first-person narrator.

NEUTRALLY OBSERVING POINT OF VIEW

The neutrally observing storyteller adopts a position somewhere between the omniscient point of view and the character-related one. The lines of demarcation are not fixed and it is not uncommon for categories to overlap. In contrast to the omniscient point of view, a neutrally observing point of view does not allow a privileged overview of all the elements of the segment of reality that is being observed. The filmmaker observes it and presents it as he finds it without intervening to give his own interpretation any more than is absolutely necessary. He is not normally present himself, since he is usually trying to reduce the "storyteller" aspect to a minimum (he is "listening" rather than "talking"). Such films often have no commentary—the filmmaker wants the situations to speak for themselves and leaves it to the spectator to interpret and draw conclusions. A typical exponent of this style in documentary films is Frederick Wiseman. Naturally, the neutrality or objectivity of this position on the part of the filmmaker is at best very limited and sometimes downright deceptive. Still, the filmmaker determines what to _exclude_, what to highlight, how to edit the material—he is still the ruler of the film's Plane of Discourse. As such, he cannot avoid putting his subjective mark on what he presents to the audience, no matter how dispassionately objective he purports to be.

EXAMPLE: Scorsese's _Taxi Driver_

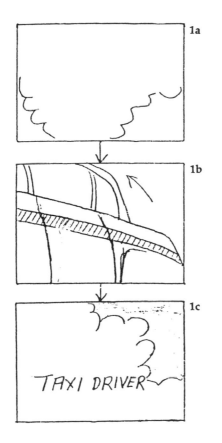

1a White smoke (exhaust fumes).

Music: dramatic

1b A yellow taxi passes.

ditto

1c White smoke fills the picture again. Credits

ditto

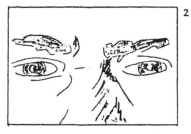

2

Big close-up of eyes.
Changes of light as if
from several neon lights.

Dreamy saxophone music

3

Blurred shapes seen
through wet
windscreen.

ditto

4

Street reflections
in the rain seen
through windscreen.

*Music becomes dramatic
again.*

5

People pass by in the street.
Slow motion.

ditto

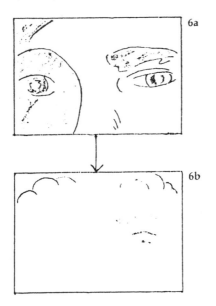

6a | Big close-up of eyes
looking from side
to side.

Dreamy saxophone music

6b | The eyes disappear
behind a cloud of smoke.

Harsher chords

Taxi Driver's opening shots establish its highly charged, subjective point of view. Through the eyes of the disoriented main character, we see New York as an oppressive nightmare, a cold, menacing city.

3

Narrative Functions
Principles of Selection
(The *Why* of Film Narrative)

Whether we are talking about the narrative elements of the Plane of Discourse or those of the Plane of Events, their particular use should be clearly justifiable in every case. Any element that does not have a clear function within the narrative framework has probably been used thoughtlessly, and the filmmaker then runs the risk of blurring the filmic expression he is trying to make.

Schematically, we can distinguish between six different types of narrative functions.

1) Realistic function
2) Dramatic function
3) Thematic function
4) Lyrical function
5) Comic function
6) Extraneous function or non-function

The use of the various narrative elements of the Plane of Events, as well as those of the Plane of Discourse, should in any particular instance be accounted for in terms of those narrative functions.

The concrete filmic expression arrived at usually serves a combination of these functions.

REALISTIC FUNCTION

Narrative elements have a realistic function when they are necessary for the communication of realistic effect. Realistic expression deepens the sense of reality, helps the audience to get their bearings, and increases credibility.

On the Plane of Events, things have a certain appearance simply because they look that way in reality. For example, if the film has a policeman, no explanation is necessary for his wearing a policeman's hat—that is what real policemen do.

When the realistic function is predominant, we wish to present to the audience an uncluttered and undistorted view of the situation (factual or fictional) that is depicted. On the Plane of Discourse, we may adopt a style that encourages the illusion of reality. Narrative means such as camera angle, picture framing and lighting are chosen so as to make as lucid a presentation as possible. The audience is invited to experience what happens on the screen in such a way that they feel they are present within the physical world that is portrayed. For instance, the use of long, unbroken takes may enhance this illusion more than a style that relies heavily on editing.

DRAMATIC FUNCTION

Narrative elements serve a dramatic function when they determine how people _act_ within the situations in which they find themselves. Dramatic elements _dynamically_ affect the course of action—they influence human relations as well as people's wishes, opinions, and choices. The dramatic elements are the motive force of the dynamic action; it is through them that the various parts of the dramatic conflict are made to hook into each other in such a way that the conflict is made to move and change.

On the Plane of Events a motive has dramatic significance if it influences the actual course of things. A knife, for instance, acquires dramatic significance if its presence in a situation determines the behavior of one or more characters, whether or not the knife is actually used. The very fact that the knife is there, ready to be used by whomever grabs it, may be the very factor that prevents a tense situation from erupting into a fight. Or it may be the decisive factor that entices an otherwise timid person to launch an attack. Clearly, if the knife were not there, things would have taken a different turn.

On the Plane of Discourse we decide, for example, to insert a close-up reaction shot of a girl who is listening to a conversation. This shot is inserted immediately after something has been said that has important consequences for the girl. The close-up has a dramatic function because it picks out and emphasizes the relevance _to the girl_ of what is said. What she has just heard is going to change the way she acts, and the close reaction shot focuses our attention on this change.

It must be pointed out that, although elements on the Plane of

Discourse can be dramatically *motivated* (i.e., the purpose of these narrative devices is to bring out and underline dramatic motives on the Plane of Events), they can never themselves be dramatically *motivating*. The implements of the Plane of Discourse can never intervene dynamically in what happens on the Plane of Events. The girl in the example above does not react to the conversation *because* she suddenly realizes she is in close-up! It is what she hears that makes her react, not the size of the shot; indeed, the size of the shot does not exist in the fictional world of which she is a part. The size of the shot only exists in the filmmaker's way of recounting the situation to his audience, i.e., only in the *communication* between filmmaker and spectator.

Some films try to give the *appearance* of dramatic action by using elaborate technical gimmicks, without actually having anything dramatic to say. These films often seem superficial and affected. The filmmaker shows off and tries to create a certain impression with the elements of the Plane of Discourse in order to hide the fact that he has nothing to say. (The Plane of Events is uninteresting and the Plane of Discourse is mere packaging.)

THEMATIC FUNCTION

A filmic expression is predominantly thematic when it acts as a *comment* on or *interpretation* of what happens on the Plane of Events. It acts as a kind of meditation on the part of the filmmaker on the story he is telling. Thematic motives cannot usually be perceived by the characters in the film—they are a message from the filmmaker to the audience regarding what the film is about. Thematic motives are often an indication of the *meaning* of what we see and hear.

We may show something on the Plane of Events without it having any visible influence on what happens; it merely throws indirect light on things and suggests ways of interpreting their meanings. For example, in an East German feature film about hospital modernization, we see two doctors discussing the consequences of the imminent installation of a new computer. During the conversation, the senior of the two, who is very enthusiastic, is trying to make a coffee machine work. He fails. The coffee machine has no dramatic function (whether the man gets his coffee or not has no dramatic significance). This little incident works *thematically* by throwing an ironic light on the relation between man and technology—it is a comment on what the doctors are discussing. This significance is not perceived by the doctors themselves, who do not make any connection between the coffee machine and the computer system. However, it seems appropriate that the film's viewers make this connection.

Notice, however, that the incident with the coffee machine also has a clear _realistic_ function; it is not only thematic. If thematic motives on the Plane of Events do not also have a natural, realistic point of reference, they often look like obtrusive symbolism. This easily becomes far-fetched and clumsy. It is much more satisfying when the symbolism (the thematic meaning) springs naturally and unlooked for from reality.

This way of creating thematic meanings on the Plane of Events is a convenient trick in countries with strict censorship (see the example above). It also lends itself very well to the cinema, since it encourages the art of concrete suggestion.

In certain instances when the camera acts independently of what happens on the Plane of Events, this may be a means of creating thematic meaning. If the camera pans (an effect on the Plane of Discourse) without following a moving subject, this is often the case (unless it is simply a matter of setting the scene, in which case the function of the pan is realistic). For example, a scene opens with the shot of the steps outside a courtroom. Here we see a judge, whom we know to be corrupt, in conspiratorial conversation with his client. After a few seconds, the camera tilts upward and comes to rest on the statue of Justice above the entrance to the building. The connection between the corrupt judge and the symbol of justice presents a _critical_ comment that only exists on the Plane of Discourse.

LYRICAL FUNCTION

The main purpose of a concrete filmic expression may be to create a particular atmosphere or feeling. Of all the various types of function, this is possibly the most difficult to master because it is usually either underestimated or overestimated. Lyrical scenes are often used as mere interludes. The danger is that lyrical effects can become an end in themselves—the lyrical expression stands out so much from the rest of the film that it creates aesthetic imbalance.

With the exception of those cases where the lyrical atmosphere is the main aim of the film, lyrical elements should provide _support_ for the dramatic or thematic elements that constitute the main thrust of the film (such as the lilacs in Sjöberg's _Miss Julie_). In other words, lyrical elements should blend organically and invisibly with other elements. On the Plane of Discourse, lyrical elements should be handled with extreme care. Effects such as slow motion, back-lighting, and extremely long telephoto shots, if not organically incorporated into the film, can throw the spectator so far out of the film that he may never find his way back.

Consistency in atmosphere is a necessity in film. The same atmosphere should be maintained (be homogenous) until a change is indicated by other fundamental motives. Disconnected, unmediated, and arbitrary changes of atmosphere are a common fault—they make the audience aware of how the filmmaker works to manipulate their emotions.

COMIC FUNCTION

We shall make no attempt to define what is comic and what is not. This would be a futile exercise. The idea, first and foremost, is to make people laugh with the film and not at it, as well as to make them laugh at the right moment. Comic relief only works if the audience really needs it.

If something is intended to be funny, it must be set up. The foundations must be laid, certain seeds must be planted before the comic effect can be achieved. When Woody Allen sneezes into the box of cocaine in *Annie Hall*, we laugh because we just learned that it cost $2,000 an ounce.

Comic effects can be created countless ways by manipulating the Plane of Discourse, and this never fails to fascinate the beginner. (How many hours have been spent in the cutting room, creating effects which, unfortunately, turn out to be pointless?) These exercises are all very well (they help us to live longer), but we must bear in mind that the effect of a comically motivated narrative device is often in inverse proportion to the ease with which the audience can see through the underlying technique.

Comic elements, like lyrical elements, work best when used in conjunction with realistic, dramatic, and/or thematic motives so that the comedy comes in unnoticed, seemingly easy and unforced. We do not laugh when we are aware of how hard someone is trying to be funny.

EXTRANEOUS FUNCTION OR NON-FUNCTION

The first thing to be said about extraneous functions is that they should never occur; the second is that they almost invariably do. For the purpose of analysis, it is extremely important to be able to isolate them, or we will never understand why films come to look the way they do. A lot of what we see in a film does not mean anything at all—it is simply there, unintended.

Extraneous motives are all the factors that influence the final result _from the outside_ and over which the filmmaker has no control. They may have financial or political reasons or they can happen quite by chance. Also, reality may not follow the rules the filmmaker expects. The true artist reveals himself in these situations by changing negative to positive, by creating sense out of nonsense.

If the hero in a film drives a Volkswagen, it _may_ be because the manufacturer has put money in the film; otherwise she/he would have a Volvo, as specified in the script. In such cases, the changes made must not be of such a nature that they affect the logic of the story or else important changes may have to be made to the script.

The following situation is quite common: You make a film and are obliged to use a jerky pan, though you cry bitter tears over the decision. The jerkiness was not intentional—there was something wrong with the tripod head (at least that is what the cameraman says). Then something happens that makes filmmaking seem worthwhile after all; a critic sees the jerky pan as a perfect expression of the instability of your hero's mind. A stroke of genius!

Far-fetched? Not at all. It happens all the time. Hitchcock's _Marnie_ has some unusually ugly backprojection effects that some critics immediately interpreted as an expression of the heroine's anxiety. Hitchcock himself was raging mad over this—the lab had done a bad job.

Another example: Bergman's _Sawdust and Tinsel_ (_Gycklarnas Afton_) has some over-exposed scenes whose expressionistic values launched Bergman on his international career. These came about because the second cameraman misread the meter. At first, Bergman was furious when he saw the results. However, he changed disaster to triumph by fading the "ruined" scenes into white instead of fading them down into black. A new style was born.

These examples show how extraneous factors can easily be interpreted as expressions of internal, thematic motives. That is what we have critics for, really; in this way the art progresses and develops. Non-narrative elements that first came about for extraneous reasons are given a thematic interpretation. In subsequent films these arbitrary effects are added to the filmmaker's arsenal and are now used as deliberate cinematic tools.

4

THE ELEMENTS OF NARRATIVE

Means of Expression in Film and TV

Both cinema and television take many of their stories from theatre and novels; the same stories are found in all three media—*the dramatic structure* can be roughly the same for them all. In other words, a story can be transposed from one medium to another, though the treatment of the story varies considerably. A good play or novel can become a bad film in spite of having basically the same dramatic structure. Good results can only be obtained by deliberately using those *means of expression* that are peculiar to film and television.

The means of expression in film and television—the elements of narrative—fall into two distinct categories: those belonging to the Plane of Events and those belonging to the Plane of Discourse.

Means of Expression on the Plane of Events (What We See and Hear)

1) Physical appearance
2) Acting
3) Costume and make-up
4) Setting
5) Props
6) Time
7) Weather
8) Physical relations

9) Movement
10) Real colors
11) Natural light
12) Real sound
13) Real music
14) Dialogue

Means of Expression on the Plane of Discourse (How We See and Hear)

15) Format
16) Shot composition
17) Focal distance and definition
18) Size of shot
19) Camera angle
20) Camera movement
21) Color and monochrome
22) Artificial light
23) Type of film and exposure
24) Special photographic effects
25) Editing
26) Sound effects
27) Film music
28) Commentary
29) Texts, subtitles, etc.
30) Title

This division does not pretend to be rigorously scientific, it simply serves as a good starting point for a systematic examination of the various narrative elements the filmmaker has at his disposal. Actually, hardly any of these elements can be considered in isolation. For example, nos. 16-20 are what we commonly call *camera treatment*, and each component must be determined according to its place in the camera treatment as a whole. Moreover, these elements of the Plane of Discourse must be determined by the events they are intended to describe, especially aspects of acting (nos. 2, 8, and 9).

PHYSICAL APPEARANCE
In the vast majority of films, people are the most important components in the story. It is vital that the actors' physical appearanc-

es should suit the roles they are playing, since every detail contributes to the characterization of the part. In film, we, the audience, are usually invited to make certain deductions from appearances—what we actually see is an indication of what lies underneath. Typecasting has led to the creation of a number of stereotypes. A tall, well-built man is expected to behave differently than a short, thin man. Even if we want to contradict these stereotype images, we must bear in mind how they work or the audience reaction will be guided by factors that are outside our control.

An ugly woman playing the part of Juliet in the world's greatest love story can only produce a comic effect. When a 300-pound Brünnhilde makes her entrance in a film of Wagner's work, it is not always easy to give credence to Siegfried's declarations of love, even if the lady's voice is divine.

Audience reaction can also be guided to a considerable extent in documentary and journalistic filming, by allowing outward appearance to be decisive when selecting representatives of different sides in a conflict.

ACTING

This category is so vast that it would be futile to attempt to discuss it in a few lines. It comprises everything the actor does on the set. However, one should bear in mind that the art of suggestion is much more effective on TV and in the cinema than a grandiose theatrical style. Here, too, inner qualities and states of mind should be suggested by means of concrete appearances—mime, looks, gesture, posture, etc. The most convincing film actors are those who have mastered *the language of the body,* a subtle combination of outward appearance and underacting. What we should aim for is economy of expression, the greatest possible effect with the least possible effort. A glance can express much more than a violent gesture.

COSTUME AND MAKE-UP

We all tend to judge by appearances. In the cinema, costume is one of the most effective tools we can use to facilitate characterization. A man's way of dressing at work and off-duty can give us an insight into his personality. Is he smart at work and unkempt at home? Does he suddenly change his style? Does his style of dress clash with other aspects of his character? In other words, is he telling lies, deliberately or otherwise, with his clothes? Why? Here again, it is important to realize how much external appearance can tell us about things that we do not actually see. Changes in make-up and hairstyle can suggest more profound inner changes. Why does a housewife suddenly begin to wear make-up and change her hairstyle after she has not done so for twenty years?

SETTING

The setting should be chosen to offer the greatest possible room for expression of the dramatic and/or thematic material of the film (the mental hospital contrasted with the sea in _One Flew Over The Cuckoo's Nest_, a film about freedom and restraint). Situations and conflicts should arise organically and in an uncontrived way, from their setting. If we find ourselves in a communist training camp (as in Gabor's _Angi Vera_), conflict must almost inevitably arise in matters of discipline, self-esteem, duty, opportunism, and so on. People appear to be real when they both reflect and react to the settings in which they are placed. Even in the rebellion against the limitations of the surroundings, we carry the surroundings with us (Jean in Sjöberg's _Miss Julie_).

Setting always has a number of expressive undertones and overtones that must be found, brought out, and made to play an active part when the feel of the film is being created. Antonioni's _The Red Desert_ would probably be unimaginable in any other setting than the dismal industrial background of Ravenna.

PROPS

The things that people surround themselves with should, ideally, contribute in a meaningful way to the telling of the story. They should be considered tools of characterization. A man who never leaves the house without first slipping a dagger into his pocket is immediately thought to be interesting. Our relationships with inanimate objects say a great deal about us. What sort of things do we collect? Which things do we avoid or dislike?

Inanimate objects can play an active and/or passive part: In a passive sense they surround people as expressions of their lives and values. A rug that is so beautiful that its owner has a fit of hysterics every time someone treads on it makes an indirect comment on the owner. Props assume an active part when someone acts with their help or as a result of their presence. _Taxi Driver_ has a decisive turn in the story when the central character acquires an arsenal; the guns become a strong motivating factor in his behavior. A well-constructed film tries as far as possible to "talk through the props" when it would otherwise be necessary to resort to explanations in the dialogue.

TIME

We associate certain events with certain times of the year. Shifts in season or in nature probably have greater significance to the story if they take place in the country rather than in the city. Many melancholy stories are set in late autumn. Christmas time, when the whole family is gathered together in enforced joy, brings about many a dramatic event. The truth slips out on Sundays. Evening's expectations are contrasted with the disappointment of morning.

WEATHER

Weather gives meaning to events in films much more than in real life. If it rains on our wedding day, we do not think that the wedding caused the rain (few people would attach any significance to it). However, if it rains at a wedding in a film, we immediately see it as something to be anxious about. Imagine the following situation filmed in two different types of weather: (1) Boy runs away with girl on a motorcycle in pouring rain. Cut to them sitting on a hillside in blazing sunshine. (2) Boy and girl run away on a motorcycle in blazing sunshine. Cut to the pair of them sitting on a hillside in pouring rain. In the first example they escape from a drab world to sweet liberty. In the second they wake up from their dream and have to face a grey, merciless world. Yet, apart from the weather, the two situations are identical.

Sometimes a scene has to be shot regardless of what the weather is like. At these times the filmmaker must be aware of how the weather influences what the audience experiences. The associations that the weather creates can determine whether or not the scene can be used. If this is not borne in mind, the audience may read unintentional meanings into the scene, with devastating results.

PHYSICAL RELATIONS

The way people are positioned in relation to one another is a narrative element that is often handled in a rather sloppy manner. Yet, here too, it is possible to impart essential information by hinting at things rather than by having to resort to the spoken word. For example, if a man boards a bus and sees that the only other passenger is a woman, it is of special significance if he sits down beside her. A person who hides in a corner at a party does not cause the same audience reaction as someone who dominates the dance floor. Some people avoid touching others while other people put their arms around everybody they meet. During a conversation, when an actor moves toward the person he is talking to, turns his back on him, or takes a step backwards, this often expresses a shift in his relationship with his interlocutor. If a person always walks to a window in every room he or she enters (as with the protagonist in Antonioni's *The Eclipse*) we try to find a meaning in his or her behavior.

MOVEMENT

When the cinema was in its infancy, the fact that the pictures moved was enough. Nowadays we are no longer satisfied with that, but still a film that does not make use of movement will be considered static. A type of film based on the extreme use of movement is farce, which continues to flourish even today, though not in the same degree as in the early days of the cinema. However, movement is not synonymous with drama, as Hemingway so aptly pointed out. Many "action films" consist simply of movement without any dramatic thread: endless car chases, running over roofs, climbing up and down the fronts of houses, and so on. Here too, it is a matter of the least possible means having the greatest effect so that when violent movement is at last triggered off, it has the desired effect. Both *French Connection* films are good examples of this.

REAL COLORS

Color is a vital aspect of the reality of events. (Even in black and white fiction films, where the black and white rendering is an effect on the Plane of Discourse, we must presume that the characters in the film experience everything in color). Although color as an element of narrative was not really considered artistically pure in the forties and fifties, today it has become one of the most sensitive instruments of artistic films. The problem with color is that it tends to beautify reality so that lyrical and pastoral tones are created where they do not belong. For this reason it is sometimes necessary to alter real colors—remove those that interfere or attract too much attention—before shooting. The *psychological* effects of color are of particular interest (red for anguish or aggression, blue for coldness, green for calm and strength) These are qualities that undoubtedly are to a great extent determined by factors of culture (e.g., the color of death is white in China and black in the West).

NATURAL LIGHT
Modern fast films and light-sensitive optics make it possible to work almost entirely in natural light. (Kubrick lit up whole palace salons in *Barry Lyndon* using only candle light.) Strongly lit objects attract more attention than weakly lit ones. This enables the filmmaker to divide the dramatic emphasis between objects and people. Shadows and darkness are usually associated with something threatening, even and soft light with goodness. Lighting people and objects from one side or from underneath produces strong shadows and creates a sensation of division or imbalance.

Gas-tube lights and other authentic sources of light that are often found in public places such as railway stations or libraries frequently produce distortions when rendered onto color film. The picture assumes an artificial, "unrealistic" appearance that the real location did not have. The audience is disposed to accept these kinds of distortions when they appear in a documentary film or in a newsreel. This is not the case in feature films. When watching documentaries, we care less about the blue light that floods into the room through the window. The unrealistic effect, caused by the difference in color temperature between daylight and artificial light, has become a documentary convention. In a feature film, the cinematographer would invariably put a red filter on the window (or a blue filter in front of the artificial light source) to even out the difference.

REAL SOUND
By "real sound" we mean all of those sounds that can be heard on the Plane of Events (with the exceptions of dialogue and music, which are considered separately). It is therefore not important whether the sound is recorded at the same time as the image or is post-synchronized; the only criterion is that it is potentially audible within the realm of the Plane of Events. Roughly speaking, there are two categories of real sound:

Effects. By this we mean significant sounds that the audience must be able to distinguish (gunshots, the telephone ringing, a ticking clock, a barking dog). Occasionally some sounds can be emphasized and given more importance than they would normally have (the *close-up sound* of the dripping tap in the long shot of Carol in Polanski's *Repulsion*).

Background atmosphere. The great importance of this lies in its capacity to enlarge the audience's experience of film space so that we feel that it expands in every direction beyond the well-defined, two-dimensional limits of the screen. Background atmosphere is generally subdued during dialogue (e.g., the murmur in a restaurant and any other non-significant sound); we are, so to speak, helped in the process of *selective listening* that we normally practice.

We can and should be as flexible in sound treatment as in visual narrative. The important thing is not that everything should be heard but that we hear what is important at any given moment.

REAL MUSIC

In many films, the only music heard is played by someone as an integral part of the action (it is part of the factual or fictional reality). Real music must appear natural and inconspicuous (e.g., the pop-music from the jukebox in the local café). The musical quality does *not* determine what constitutes good or bad real music but rather whether or not it reflects, characterizes or comments on the people, the places, and the events. For this purpose, a simple song can be much more suitable than Bruckner's Ninth.

Real music is often used as an ironic commentary—for example, the "Hallelujah Chorus" during the beggars' orgy in Bunuel's *Viridiana*. This use of music—known as counterpoint technique—works best when it is closely linked to events (and consequently has a realistic function); it is more than a superficial "more knowledgeable than thou" comment from the director. If the irony is in the setting, it is as if reality itself were to reveal its own truth.

DIALOGUE

One good way of testing a film is to turn off the sound altogether and see how much you understand simply by looking at the images. If you understand nothing at all, the film might possibly be a Norwegian or Swedish "art film." We resort far too often to dialogue to communicate what we cannot manage to do with images and events. *Explanatory* dialogue (the crutches a screenwriter grabs when he can no longer walk—i.e., write) is the villain in the majority of failed cinema dramas. One golden rule to be borne in mind immediately is that *dialogue should not determine the drama but should spring organically from it.* In other words, *the dialogue must be a function of the characters and their situation.*

The form and function of dialogue will be further considered later.

FORMAT

The choice of film format has a bearing on how other elements of narrative will be treated. If we use electronics, obviously the best bet is a normal television format (roughly the same as the classic "Academy" screen format). There are many different formats in film, but for the sake of simplicity, we shall merely make a distinction between Academy and wide-screen format. The wide-screen makes new demands above all on shot composition and cutting. This format opened up film space in the horizontal plane and made it possible to treat several elements of action at the same time. This was to the advantage of realistic presentation. The ability to make a sweeping appraisal of the scene was enhanced. However, at the same time, cutting became more difficult since several different elements had to tally in each cut. From this came a tendency toward longer takes with greater internal dynamic content.

Mention must also be made of the 70mm and Cinerama formats. These have most often been used for highly spectacular purposes, but they also include examples of creative, artistic motives for the choice of format—Kubrick's *2001* and Tarkovsky's *Solaris* both make full use of every square inch of the large screen.

SHOT COMPOSITION

The composition of the shot is linked inseparably with the positioning of actors (cf., physical relations on the Plane of Events) although they are not exactly the same thing. *The relationship to the camera* is not part of people's experience of reality (except in certain factual programs where the camera plays an active part). The composed *image* exists only as an element on the Plane of Discourse. The camera does not influence the action, but merely the spectator's experience of it. This influence can be brought about in many ways, such as by allowing one person to fill a great part of the screen. Things that are visually dominant attract attention and, in order to create this effect, the distance of the camera from the subject is just as important as the subject's natural size. If, in the foreground, we see the face of a little boy, staring anxiously past the camera and, in the background, a full-length image of a man talking to him, the dramatic emphasis is on the boy—his reaction is more important than what the man is saying. A director can say a great deal about the relationships between characters by simply manipulating their positions with regard to the camera and the picture frame. Antonioni's _The Outcry_ has one scene where a man and a woman dominate one half of the screen each; between them, in the background—behind a window—we see their daughter staring toward them. The two adults have drifted apart from one another; the daughter, who once bound them together, stands between them now to complicate matters. This thematic comment lies entirely in the composition of the shot.

People usually find that horizontal lines create a greater feeling of calm than vertical lines. Diagonals produce dynamism, depth of picture, and a sense of movement. Asymmetrical composition causes imbalance. Lack of "air" around characters can cause a claustrophobic effect (this is often used in horror films).

We can derive a greater insight into shot composition if we study the history of painting.

FOCAL DISTANCE AND DEFINITION

Choice of focal distance must be consistent throughout the film. That is to say, it must be subject to a dominating _narrative style_. The focal distance should express the director's attitude toward the story he is telling. Films that aimlessly and unsystematically throw the spectator back and forth from one focal distance to another often seem to have neither form nor style. The spectator has no point of reference. A director such as Stanley Kubrick composes almost all his shots with a wide-angle lens. This gives his films an air of coolness and distance. The shorter focal distance increases the depth of field and gives an extended account of the setting. This allows Kubrick to work with more complex compositions, which give a great effect of depth. The wide-angle lens also increases the apparent distance between foreground and background, creates artificial contrasts in size, and distorts the subject when the distance from the camera is short. All this can be instrumental in helping the director to shape the stylistic outlook of the film. We can say, then, that the wide angle encourages a thematic and realistic film narrative. The spectator is invited to observe events that occur simultaneously and to glean meanings that would not be apparent if each event were shown separately. The "deep focus" style used in the forties and fifties by Welles and Wyler was intended as an aid to realism; the spectator should not merely look at a picture, he should enter into the illusory three dimensions of the image itself.

Cinematographer Jörgen Persson's *Elvira Madigan* style can be said to illustrate the other extreme. Powerful telephoto lenses isolate the subject from both surroundings and background, diminish picture space, and narrow our visual field. The reduced depth of field allows what is in front of the subject as well as what is behind it to come out of focus. Long focal distances are well suited for impressionistic-lyrical films.

Great care must be taken with *visible changes of focus*. For instance, focus is changed from a person speaking in the foreground to another who is listening in the background (the person out of focus is blurred). The shift of focus draws the spectator's attention to the technique itself and can therefore be seen as alienating and artificial.

The same can be said of a lens with *variable focal distance (zoom)*. Zooming is often used instead of tracking, but the results are always more artificial. Zooming in is rather like pointing, almost as if the photographer were to put his hand in front of the lens and point at whatever it is he wants the audience to look at. Zooming out is easier to justify—it reveals the context of a detail. Even when we try to exercise restraint (some people find it impossible *not* to zoom), the increased freedom in the choice of focal length can easily lead to a certain laxity and inconsistency in style.

SIZE OF SHOT

By this we mean the size of the subject in relation to the frame. A great number of gradations are possible but we normally make the following divisions: *very long shot, long shot, medium shot, close-up,* and *big close-up*. A conventional film, which is easy to follow, constructs its scenes using all the various shot sizes. In this case the arrangement follows a logic that comprises the following steps:

establish, present, emphasize. These, in brief, tell the audience the _where, who,_ and _what_ of the film.

Establish: We need to know where we are and to acquaint ourselves with the physical surroundings in order to have an idea of where different things are in relation to each other. This is where the _very long shot_ (establishing shot) comes in—it shows the scene and the physical relationships in their entirety.

Present: Assuming that the scene deals with people, we want to know who is involved. The very long shot does not indicate anyone in particular; we need to get a closer look, usually by way of _long shots_ or _medium shots_ that show clearly the physical characteristics of the people involved. The long shot shows the person from head to toe and the medium shot from the knees up.

Emphasize: If we want to bring out something that is dramatically or thematically essential, the easiest way to do it is with a _close-up._ The close-up is a very dynamic instrument that is often used to start the action going. A close-up usually demands some kind of reaction, some- thing that happens as a consequence; when something is brought out very clearly we expect it to have significance for what happens afterward.

A simple example of the above: _Where_ are we? In a bank. (Very long shot.) _Who_ can we see? A tall, well-dressed woman at the counter. (Long shot or medium shot.) _What_ is she doing? She's taking a pistol from her handbag. (Close-up.) The action has begun.

This can, of course, be done in reverse order: first showing the detail, then the person, then the whole scene. This makes the audience more curious—the information is rationed so that each shot in turn answers a question the audience is asking. But sooner or later we must establish the scene, often more than once. Nothing is more boring than a film consisting entirely of medium shots and close-ups. The geographical confusion can obscure even the simplest of actions. Besides, the close-up loses all its dramatic weight. Many TV plays are ruined by this anti-dramatic, insipid technique.

Anyone who would like to learn how to vary image size to good dramatic effect can learn a great deal from Alfred Hitchcock.

The close-up is not only dramatically sensitive, it must also be used with great care from the thematic point of view. It often feels like an importunate intrusion. Antonioni's _The Night_ has a close-up of Jeanne Moreau's hand, wearing a wedding ring, scratching the plaster from the wall of a tumbledown house. One easily feels that the symbolism is exaggerated. The close-up is always, in a certain sense, an abstraction—it isolates detail and removes the organic context. When, in addition, this abstraction has an extra thematic/metaphoric meaning, the shot must be *very* well motivated if it is to succeed.

Instead of cutting between different image sizes, the camera treatment can be arranged to make it possible to go from one size to another in the same take. This technique often feels more elegant, livelier, more sensuous. This has become something of a distinguishing mark in good Hungarian films. (One outstanding example is Gabor's *Angi Vera.*)

Realistic films (e.g., the Italian neo-realist films) usually stick to the larger images. Long shots and very long shots prevail (and, to a certain extent, medium shots). In these films, people are usually seen as a function of their environment and cannot, therefore, be isolated from it. It is less common for a film to be wholly constructed with very long shots, but this was, in fact, the case with Angelopoulos' *The Travelling Players* a historical-political fresco nearly four hours long.

CAMERA ANGLE

The choice of camera angle is linked intimately to the perspective of the storyteller, i.e., the narrative point of view. When adopting a *neutrally observing point of view,* the filmmaker should restrict himself to camera angles that allow the subject to appear in as unremarkable a light as possible. The best angle is often one that can present the subject or the action in the clearest and most distinct way from a natural spectator position. This usually means from a natural eye height. The *character-related point of view* also uses subjective shots (P.O.V. shots) where the camera "sees" the same as the person, from exactly the same physical vantage point. When adopting an *omniscient point of view,* the filmmaker probably enjoys most freedom because he can observe subject and action from every possible angle and often makes use of the camera angle to comment on what he sees. Bear in mind, however, that every *unnatural* camera angle works thematically; if we see something from an unexpected or unusual angle, we expect it to *mean* something special. If we see no such meaning, we find the angle false or affected. However, camera angles that deviate *slightly* from normal can help us see things more clearly. We see things in a different way and, quite literally, discover new sides of it. One director who often works in this way is Michelangelo Antonioni.

According to convention, a very high camera angle (bird's-eye view) makes the subject seem small and insignificant, while a low angle (worm's-eye view) gives the subject an air of strength and superiority. Moreover, the high angle often gives the impression that people are unwillingly stuck in or guided by circumstances, or their fate—for example, the famous very long shot in Hitchcock's _The Birds_ of the burning town, where the birds suddenly fly into the foreground of the picture and swoop down on the town, shrieking.

Further consideration of the camera angle in relation to the _line of interest_ ("the 180° axis") will be given elsewhere.

CAMERA MOVEMENT

In principle, there are two _kinds_ of camera movement—movements that _follow_ a moving subject and movements that are not determined by movements on the Plane of Events. The first type is often motivated completely by a desire to follow the dramatic action. (The man walks from his chair to the window and the camera follows him.) The second type usually has a meaningful function, a thematic link or association is made between different objects or events. (The camera pans from the couple dancing to the girl sitting alone in a corner.) In the latter case, the movement is made deliberately noticeable in a way that is not the case when the camera movement is "covered" by a moving subject. By means of thematic camera movements the director reminds us that he is the one guiding the story.

The number of camera movements depends very much on the cutting style. The shorter the time between cuts, the less the need to move the camera. (In Eisenstein's thematically cut films, the camera hardly moves at all.) We find the contrary in films with long and dynamic scenes—the camera in constant movement prevents the scenes from becoming static. (The Hungarian filmmaker Miklos Jancso is the foremost exponent of this type of film—his _Electra_, the most extreme of his films, has only eleven cuts.)

Camera movements—especially _tracking_—have in themselves enormous power when it comes to creating "feel" and atmosphere (the tracking shots in Resnais' _Hiroshima Mon Amour_ are prime examples). Tracking also has a capacity that is difficult to define but which suggests the transient nature of things. Consider, for example, all the films where a *journey* expresses underlying psychological or existential changes (Antonioni's *The Adventure* and *The Passenger*, Kawalerowicz's *Night Train*).

The main difference between tracking in and zooming seems to be that tracking pulls the spectator into the picture in a way that feels almost physical. Zooming merely brings out the detail. Tracking increases the sense of presence and realism, while the zoom increases the feeling that the director is playing for effects.

Another way of increasing the feeling of realism is to use a hand-held camera. This has its most natural place in documentary or pseudo-documentary films, to give the spectator the illusion of looking at an authentic reality (Pontecorvos's *The Battle of Algiers*).

COLOR EFFECTS AND MONOCHROME

By color effects we mean all of the colors in the completed film that are not to be found in the actual scene. These effects can be created, for example, with the help of color filters or colored lights. Color effects are often used to give certain scenes a *tone*. This can be observed in two scenes from Bergman's *A Passion*. In one scene, Max von Sydow and Bibi Andersson go to bed together. It is evening, the atmosphere is sensual, the light has a warm, reddish tone. The following morning, when they wake up from the spell, the light has become an unpleasant blue, piercing and unromantic. The warmth has changed to disillusion and coldness.

Before the days of color film, *tinting* was often used to suggest a dominant emotional tone. Blue for night, red for dusk, pink for love, etc. This type of effect is very rare today in feature films, though in television, especially in light entertainment, it sometimes occurs as an electronic device. However, this is used more for sensuous effect than as a thematic means of expression.

Monochrome also has its rightful place in this category, since the black-and-white effect exists *only* as a device on the Plane of Discourse. Regrettably, black-and-white film has lost ground for the sake of realism. The limits inherent in monochrome also presented a challenge to the filmmaker to refine his expressive means. Of course, color film means that the artist has one more creative element to work with, but if he does not use color as a formative component of his adopted style, he may as well do without it. In this case color simply dilutes artistic expression.

ARTIFICIAL LIGHT

By and large, the same can be said of artificial light as of natural light. The minimal demand is that the film should be exposed, and documentary films often have neither the time nor the opportunity to expect any more than that. But only a singularly unambitious feature film would not aim higher. A Swedish photographer has said that the art lies not in placing light, but rather in taking light away. The overruling ambition should be to form things with light as a painter forms things with his brush.

The decisive factor in whether or not we work with realistic light is the narrative style. Realistic light does not attract attention (in other words it has no thematic significance). The lighting is arranged to support or to suggest the natural light source (windows, a chandelier). Expressionistic films (such as many of Bergman's films or Sjöberg's _Miss Julie_) often ignore such considerations and manipulate the light in order to create psychological and thematic values. Horror films often excel in this.

An important distinction can be made between _high key_ and _low key_ lighting. High key means that the scene is more or less completely lit and contrasts in light are minimal. This was one of the earmarks of early color films (e.g., American musicals) and is now common in most series produced for television. (_Dallas_ is a typical example. The whole set is lit so that the camera can change position quickly without being hampered by the lighting arrangement.) High key lighting often has a flat, artificial look. Low key means that the contrasts between light and dark are brought out. Often only people and important objects are clearly lit while the surroundings are in shade and semi-darkness. A masterful example of low key lighting to simulate natural light can be seen in Gabor's _Angi Vera_—every image reminds us of a Rembrandt painting.

FILM STOCK AND EXPOSURE

In documentaries, the choice of film stock is determined by the nature of the situations and light conditions that are expected to arise. The fast color films at our disposal today have enabled us to avoid artificial light under difficult conditions. Furthermore, fast film stocks have made it possible for us to avoid not only the sometimes unintentionally contrived effects of artificial light. Equally important, we may now eliminate the often stifling effect that a heavy, laborious technical apparatus may have in certain sensitive situations. The same holds true, of course, for light-sensitive TV cameras. The ease of shooting immediately lends itself to a narrative style that flows easily and unobtrusively, carrying the conviction of reality itself unfolding in front of the camera.

Speed, grain, and contrast range are the most important factors to consider when choosing film. The black-and-white high-contrast film used in *The Battle of Algiers* gives the film much of its widely acclaimed "realistic" effect—it looks like a documentary film although every shot is pre-arranged. Films that deal with more delicate moods tend to use a more subtle, finer-grained film.

Sometimes a faster film is used so that the filmmaker can stop down and maintain the depth of field necessary for the style of the film.

If we ignore the cases of accidental overexposure or underexposure that can occur in practice, these effects can be used as deliberate narrative means in the film. Dream scenes are often markedly overexposed, while slight underexposure can produce the effect of evening in a scene shot in daylight.

The choice between *forced processing* and changing to a faster type of film must be determined by the overall photographic style of the film. Certain types of film lend themselves to forced processing and can be mixed with others to good effect. This is not possible with all film types.

Pre-exposure can in some cases give the film a soft, pastel character.

SPECIAL PHOTOGRAPHIC EFFECTS

Fast motion usually produces a comic effect but is occasionally used to give an impression of high speed—such as in car chases. *Slow motion* gives a dream-like, romantic effect but can easily degenerate into affectation. With the help of *stop motion*, we can study certain natural processes—such as the petals growing on a flower.

Double exposure can describe a state of unreality, as in Sjöström's *The Phantom Carriage*, while *dissolving or fading* often indicates a lengthier gap in time or in events. Printer effects such as the *freeze frame* can emphasize an important moment and are often used as the last picture in a film. *Still photographs* are often used in documentary films, especially in those that reconstruct historical events.

Front or back projection is a possible solution when it would be too difficult, dangerous, or expensive to shoot on the real location. Nowadays these techniques require a great deal of control and precision in order to convince the audiences, who have become much more demanding when it comes to the technical quality of effects such as these.

Travelling matte and _chroma key_ are indispensable aids in science-fiction films and many entertainment programs on TV.

Split screen shows two separate events in the same picture, often to ironic effect (Woody Allen and Diane Keaton on their respective psychiatrist's couch in _Annie Hall_).

EDITING

Editing will be dealt with in more detail later; here we shall simply consider one or two important aspects.

Invisible cutting: The audience is not aware of the cut; two shots are joined in such a way that they give the impression of an uninterrupted sequence. This is called _continuity cutting_. The original complete situation, which could have been shot in one take, is divided into several takes that are pieced together to create the impression of completeness and indivisibility. In other words, we give the illusion of

- unity of _action_
- unity of _space_
- unity of _time_

The edited version is not a copy of reality but a _reconstruction_ based on pure illusion. The principle also applies to documentary and journalistic films.

Visible cutting: The audience is aware of the cut, either because it indicates a marked shift in place and/or time or because the joining together of shots in this way creates new _meanings_. Antonioni's _The Passenger_ has a scene where Maria Schneider tells Jack Nicholson that someone believes he is in danger. "In danger of what?" asks Nicholson and the film cuts to a crossroads where an old man is seated, leaning against a big white cross. Nicholson asks the way but, naturally, receives no reply.

In those cases where the cut is emphasized and no attempt is made to hide it, rather it is emphasized, understanding the scene depends on our ability as spectators to put the pieces together in the way intended. _Cross cutting_, for example, between rich and poor milieus may contain no continuity cuts, but since the film cuts constantly from a motif in one setting that is associated or contrasted with a motif in the other, a contradictory unity that arises out of the contrasts is created.

EFFECT SOUND

By this we mean sounds that are not part of the events portrayed—sounds that are heard by the audience and not by the characters in the film. Sometimes it is difficult to decide which is really the case. This is explained by the fact that the real sounds do not come only from the factual or fictional situation that is *visible* on the screen; sound is often of great help in enabling the audience to understand what happens *off screen.* For example, in Fassbinder's *The Marriage of Maria Braun* we hear the rattle of a machine gun and the sound of a child crying during the opening credits. Is this "real sound" or effect sound? It is purely a matter of interpretation; the sounds *could* at least exist on the Plane of Events. However, in some cases, the effect sounds are clearly unrealistic (the sound of walls splitting in Polanski's *Repulsion*). The type of film that makes the most calculated use of effect sound is perhaps the horror film since a *hint* at something we cannot actually see is important here. In this case, the sounds have their frightening effect because we do not know whether they are real or not real.

FILM MUSIC

The purpose of adding music to films is usually to underscore and increase the emotional content of the images. During the first twenty to thirty years of talking pictures, a couple could rarely kiss without being accompanied by the sound of soft strings (this was especially true of American films). Different types of music evolved for different situations, and they soon became recognizable cliches. (Here come the violins—now they are going to kiss!) This could often degenerate into musical mushiness, and the music literally told the audience what to feel. This use of music can be treacherous because the music can easily become a dramatic *substitute.* The situations themselves are lacking in dramatic nerve so the music is poured on to suggest the drama. (The music is menacing, feel how exciting it is, dear audience!) We can still see examples of this kind of playing for effect in certain TV series and so-called action films (where action often means violent physical activity and nothing else). The intention, then, should be to _underscore_, not to replace. The best music is often not noticed during the film, but is simply there as a natural and integrated part of the expression of emotions.

Music can often be used to establish the time and place of the action. We know we are in the forties when we hear Glenn Miller's "Midnight Serenade" over the credits in Nichols' _Carnal Knowledge._

The filmmaker can also use music as a subtle instrument to comment on what is happening; in other words, the music creates thematic associations. In one scene from _Miss Julie_ we hear references to Chopin's Funeral March and Mendelssohn's Wedding March; we know that the mother is dead and that an engagement is in the offing—no words are needed to tell us this. The use of music may be a sort of _counterpoint_—the music plays a role that is fairly independent in relation to the images and the events they show. The music does not say the same things as the images; it has a distancing effect in relation to the events portrayed (as in Kubrick's _Barry Lyndon_).

We must be very careful when choosing music. For example, classical music that isn't written specifically for the film, may cause strong and incorrect associations in the audience. A certain piece of music may have personal connotations that are not intended by the filmmaker.

Great care must be taken with songs. A song must never be heard at the same time as dialogue or song and dialogue cancel each other out. We listen to one or the other, and if they clash we understand neither of them.

COMMENTARY

In feature films:
In a dramatic feature film, the extensive use of a commentator is often a sign that no satisfactory solution has been found to the problems of dramatic structure. Disconnected shifts in development, unclear characterization, gaps in the logical build-up make it necessary to _explain_ to the audience what they are seeing so as not to leave too many loose ends. The technique is easier to justify when a first-person narrator expresses the thoughts of one of the characters in the film. The first-person narrator works best if he is allowed to be completely subjective; his comments are no more true or reliable than anyone else's—they may even be quite

wrong. (He does not need to express the *filmmaker's* opinions and values, which may be *critical* of the first-person narrator.)

Commentary has a more natural place in *epic films*; one characteristic of this type of film is that the story is *told* by someone who stands removed from the events. The epic perspective often takes the form of a *reflection* or *examination* of a phenomenon or an event, the outcome of which is often already known. In this case the commentary acts as an interpretation of events (as in Sanders-Brahms' *Germany, Pale Mother*). The commentary can also be ironic and playful, as in Richardson's *Tom Jones*. It is often used to link up parts of a film whose action is spread over a long period of time and is composed of a series of episodes (Ford's *Cheyenne Autumn* or Hawks' *The Big Sky*). The commentary in Truffaut's *Jules et Jim* liberates the visual flow of the film, allowing free range for the director's impressionistic fancy.

In documentary films:

The most important thing to try to avoid in documentary films is unnecessary duplication of information already contained in the pictures. The commentary should give necessary information where the pictures themselves are not enough. Moreover, it should give a personal interpretation and should pose questions. *Too many words* are lethal (after a while the audience does not understand anything). The commentary works best when administered in small doses. The concrete content of the images should speak for itself as far as possible. Where appropriate, the commentary should offer clarification and answer questions by means of a summary or comment. Many documentary films would be better with no commentary at all.

In other factual programs:

In reports and news broadcasts, the commentary is all-important. It should, as far as possible, refer to what is *concrete and specific*. Completely abstract accounts rarely remain in memory.

TEXTS, SUBTITLES, ETC.

Written texts are sometimes used at the beginning or the end of a film. When they occur at the beginning, they often give an indication of the time and place where the film is set ("London 1812," "A town in France before the Revolution"), or they give a thematic clue—often with moral overtones (as in Fuller's *Shock Corridor*.

"Whom the Gods will destroy, they first make mad."—Euripides).
When placed at the end of the film, they often give a brief account
of what happened to the protagonists later (as in Bergman's *Face
to Face* where we learn that the central character left her job and
went to the USA. This latter practice is especially common when
the film is based on a true story (as in Parker's *Midnight Express*).

Texts are sometimes used to divide the film into "chapters."
(Kub-rick's *2001* is divided under the titles "The Dawn of Man,"
"The Voyage to Jupiter" and "Beyond the Infinite") Or an affection-
ate allusion is made to the infancy of the cinema as, for example,
in Mel Brooks' *Silent Movie.*

In news broadcasts and other factual programs, texts are indispensable for quick and effective transmission of information
(names, statistics). In this same category we can also include dia-
grams and other graphics—very useful tools in informative films.

Credits are often placed after the action of the film has begun
so that a "teaser" or "hook" has time to capture the imagination of
the audience. Presumably this is a result of TV distribution.

TITLE

Finding the right title can make or break a film or a TV program.
The title should have some thematic relevance, even though it may
be a cryptic clue to the theme of the film. We should also try to
find a title that itself arouses curiosity. If we make a program about
wife-beating in Sweden and call it *Wife-Beating in Sweden*, it
sounds like a government report. If, however, we call it *It Happens
in the Best of Families*, we arouse curiosity. *What* happens? The
program provides the answer. Tune in and find out.

The problem of translating titles is a delicate one. Sometimes
it is best to keep the original. Loach's *Family Life* played to full
houses in Sweden without the title being translated. In Norway it
was called *The Case of Janice* and did not go very well. When
Antonioni's *L'éclisse* (*The Eclipse*) was given the title *Feber* (*Fever*)
in Sweden and Norway, we wondered whether it was an attempt
on the part of the distributors to relegate Antonioni to the sickbed,
where they perhaps thought he belonged.

5
AUDIO-VISUAL
NARRATIVE
The "Language" of Film and TV

A heated discussion sometimes arises between "pure" film people and people working within the electronics media (video and TV) concerning the specific nature of the respective media. Is there a *basic* difference between film and television? Do they communicate to the audience in fundamentally different ways? Needless to say, the *technical* basis of the two media is not the same. But that is not what concerns us here. The question is, Does the difference in technical origin and make-up imply that we are dealing with two very different audio-visual "languages"?

We shall not offer an incontrovertible "yes" or "no" to this question here. Our attitude, however, is that the same basic rules of narrative apply to film as well as to television. The rules of audio-visual narrative developed in film were later adopted, and—to some extent—modified, by television. The basic "grammar" (the rules of screen geography and continuity) is the same in the two media. When discussing the ground rules, we shall therefore refer sometimes to film, sometimes to TV.

It is not a matter of indifference, of course, whether the product we are making is intended for a big movie theatre or a small TV screen. The choice of medium will influence the style of the product, the number of close-ups, the kind of lighting, the style of cutting. Kubrick's *2001 does* look different on TV. But the *basic* rules of narrative are still the same.

There *is*, however, an important difference between one-camera and multi-camera techniques. The demands of a "live" multi-camera transmission will force the program makers to approach the problems of screen geography and cutting in a way that is peculiar to this form of transmission. However, in order not to create confusion, the basic rules of one-camera film or TV production will usually be followed as closely as possible.

In this study, we shall restrict ourselves to the rules of one-camera techniques.

FICTION AND DOCUMENTARY: "THE NARRATIVE APPROACH"

It will be the contention of this study that all audio-visual programs, whether fact or fiction, are _narrated_ in some way or other. Whether the situation portrayed be fiction (invented by the filmmaker) or fact (taken from a real situation outside the control of the program maker), the _way_ in which this situation is conveyed to the audience will necessarily bear the stamp of the film or program maker. We can portray invented realities and tell invented stories, or we can tell stories about situations and facts that are not of our making. Whether making a feature film or a news report, we are relating stories.

A portrayal of reality through film or TV is not and _can never be_ identical to the original situation we wish to convey. We can never eradicate ourselves as program makers. We constantly make choices as to _how_ to portray the situations in question. It cannot be otherwise. The totality of elements that constitute the Plane of Events (the situation being reported) cannot at any time be represented by the camera. _The camera will always exclude more than it reveals_. It puts reality into a two-dimensional, rectangular frame. We edit the bits and pieces we pick out in a certain order. In other words, no matter how "objective" we try to be, we cannot avoid working by way of a _Plane of Discourse_ (camera angles, camera movements, framing, editing, etc.), and this invariably creates _meanings_ that were not a part of the original situation. The report becomes our _story_ of the situation, that is to say our structured interpretation of it. Whenever we are putting pieces of film together to make a meaningful, comprehensible, logical sequence, we are _narrating_ something—fact or fiction. By way of the Plane of Discourse, we are relating stories.

IMAGE AND SOUND

When we are putting together an *audio-visual* narrative, we must bear in mind that the two elements, image and sound, work in a special way when they operate *together*. This is very different from how they work in isolation (e.g., a radio program or a written news-paper article with illustrations) because of the different speeds by which the eye and the ear perceive things, as well as how we com-pensate for the lack of the other source of information when we are, for instance, listening to the radio (only sound) or reading a news magazine (only visuals). When listening to a radio play, we create images in our heads, and these images are in perfect har-mony with what we hear. (That is why some not-so-successful films or TV programs should be "seen" on the radio!) When reading an article or a book, our attitude is wholly *reflective*—the written word substituting for sound, which we are not aware of missing.

Research into this new science is still in its infancy and we must be careful not to make overly sweeping generalizations. Howev-er, scientists seem to have a general consensus that image and sound have very different capacities when conveying information and when conveying emotion. Schematically, we can view the communicative capacity of image and sound, *when working togeth-er*, like this:

	IMAGE	SOUND
INFORMATION	70%	30%
EMOTION	30%	70%

This needs a few words of comment. Let us look at the *informa-tion* aspect first. If we let a cross-section of the normal population view a number of audio-visual information programs, we know that 70% of the information they pick up and remember will be taken from the visuals and 30% will be from the soundtrack. At least part of the reason for this is the fact that the brain processes and stores visual information much more quickly than auditory information. The latter, in order to be understood, needs more time for reflec-tive treatment. Thus, it goes without saying that a TV news pro-gram that conveys 90% of its information through the spoken word does not even try to use the medium in an effective way.

Sound, on the other hand, seems to have the capacity to work directly on our *emotions* in a way that the image does not. For example, in a famous news report from the infancy of Swedish television, a commentator drones on, in a dry, monotonous voice, about a new dental-care reform, quoting statistics half the time. On the screen we see a woman being treated for a cavity in one of her teeth. _The moment we hear the drill_, we squirm in our seats and we no longer pick up a word of what the commentator is saying. We do, however, notice the _tone_ of his voice, which is flat and uninvolved in what he is saying.

It is, perhaps, for the reasons indicated above that we so quickly adopt a cool, non-responsive attitude to the images of war, violence, misery, and suffering that constantly attack us from the TV screen. When, however, these images are accompanied by the sounds of people crying or screaming in pain, we do indeed react, no matter how many times we have heard it before.

Sound seems to work more directly and unconsciously on our emotions than does the image. This provides the enormous power for manipulation that is inherent in the audio-visual media. This effect of the medium can be counteracted only when we are aware of how image and sound really work together.

FROM THE CONCRETE TO THE ABSTRACT

Seeing is believing. It is so in our everyday life and it is so when we watch film or TV. If someone points to the floor and tells us that a big yellow spider is crawling toward us, we think he is either hallucinating or making fun of us if we do not ourselves _see_ a yellow spider there. However, if we do see a yellow spider and the other person tells us it cannot be so because there simply are no yellow spiders, we will take quick action anyway. Our survival depends on it. If we can no longer trust the evidence of our own senses, we suspect we are going mad. When we see something, we believe it. When someone just tells us about it, we can choose to believe him or we may choose to think he is telling a lie.

Audio-visual media works the same way. When the camera shows us something, it is unquestionably _there_—it is real, it is true. That is the strength of the visual image. However, our _understanding_ of what we see may be totally false. That is because an image alone tells us nothing about its _context_. Therein lies the weakness of the image. It may be taken from one context and put in another where it does not belong. When seeing an image, we very often need additional information in order to grasp the whole of which it is part.

Nevertheless, in order to be convincing, a film or a TV program must work, first of all, by way of its concrete images. If it does not, we simply feel that the documentation is not there.

Example: A documentary film about overpopulation in the Third World opens by showing us fragmented, disconnected images of congested traffic and slums in four southeast Asian cities. The commentator goes on at length to tell us, mostly by way of statistics, how the cities are growing at an uncontrollable pace, why it is so, and what the consequences will be before the year 2000. The argument is wholly abstract—it would stand just as well by itself, without the images. The images, on the other hand, mean very little on their own. The shots of slums and congested traffic *might* have been taken from any other city in the world, and the argument of the film would still be the same. Here, the images merely serve as more or less relevant *illustrations* of what the commentator is talking about. The abstract, verbal argument comes first, the concrete images come second. This is a very common journalistic mistake.

This is not just a question of communicative efficiency. What is in question here is one's attitude toward concrete reality itself. In the above case, four very dissimilar cities (Bangkok, Kuala Lumpur, Singapore, and Jakarta) are treated one and the same as if the differences between them are unimportant. This is blatantly false. The four cities could not be more dissimilar, as anyone knows who has been there. When the verbally erudite journalist works in this way, he transforms reality itself into a meaningless abstraction whose only value is that of illustrating an abstract argument. He might just as well have written a textbook.

However, one scene in the above-mentioned film shows us what it is all about. A freight train passes through a Bangkok slum. Children are playing close by the tracks. Some of them run alongside the moving train, jump on to it, and hang on with hands and feet before finally letting go and falling only inches away from the deadly wheels. Luckily, the commentator has enough sense to keep his mouth shut during this scene. The situation speaks for itself— and how! We are thrown into a very concrete and specific reality. We ask ourselves the question, How is it possible that children are left to play in an environment like this? We are intrigued, shocked. We want an answer. *Now* the commentator may come in and explain the situation to us, drawing *general* conclusions from the *specific* example. Yet the power of his argument will rest on the fact that he *first* leads us into a segment of reality that is concrete, individual, specific. The real situation portrayed focuses the problem; it forces us, the audience, to ask questions. Now—and only now!—the commentator can supply us with more generalized abstractions that *answer* our questions. The images alone, concrete and specific as they are, cannot do that. Verbal explanations can.

The rule, then, is to go from the concrete and specific to the abstract and general, not the other way round. First you show, then you explain.

One documentary filmmaker who has mastered this technique to perfection is David Attenborough. In the opening shots of the jungle episode of his *Living Planet* series, we find ourselves in the middle of the rain forest. Somebody—we only see his hands and feet—is climbing a gigantic tree. As he progresses, we see glimpses of animal and bird life, as if seen through his eyes. Nothing is explained yet, but we are unquestionably *there*, in an exciting new environment. *Then* we see Mr. Attenborough, perched on a branch high up in the canopy of the forest. He starts talking about the surrounding forest, telling us things which the images alone cannot tell. And *while* he is talking, the visual information remains virtually unchanged. Another commentator takes over, telling us how the rain forest is distributed over the face of the Earth. Then we are back with Mr. Attenborough, who introduces us to new concrete phenomena that, in their turn, demand new abstract explanations.

Documentation before explanation. Concrete before abstract. The image, which is always concrete and specific, constantly arouses our curiosity. The accomplished filmmaker knows exactly *when* to supply the (abstract) answers. His explanations *expand* from the individual case, not the other way round. That way, his audience will enjoy, remember, and *understand.*

NARRATIVE EFFICIENCY: THE USE OF METONYMY

No matter how thorough we try to be in our portrayal of some aspect of reality, we can never hope to actually *show* more than a small *part* of the circumscribed whole we want to convey. As mentioned above, the nature of the medium dictates that the camera will always, at any given moment, exclude more than it reveals. This is so even in the simplest of situations. There is no way we can convey the *whole* situation as it was in its original three-dimensional form. We must try to *suggest* the whole in such a way that the audience get the impression they are not missing anything.

As an audience, we are used to reading images in this way. When we see the image of a hand firing a gun, we do not wonder how the hand could fire the gun all by itself. We create, in our minds, the whole human being who is present outside the picture frame. (This technique of letting a part represent the whole is called, in literary theory, *synecdoche.*) In the cinema and on TV, we use this technique all the time in order to create, in the audience, the experience of situations that were never actually happening at the time of the shooting. If we position an actor against a white wall in a film studio, put a bunch of roses in his hands, then frame him in a medium shot as he is anxiously looking left and right for someone, while on the soundtrack we hear the buzz of people walking and talking and a loudspeaker voice requesting passengers booked for flight 074 to Paris to proceed to gate no. 5, we know the person is in the passenger terminal of an airport. We do not need to actually *see* the terminal; image and sound give us enough *clues* to subconsciously put the terminal together in our heads.

However, there is a more elaborate way in which the filmmaker may *represent* the whole through images that *stand for* much more than the mere physical qualities of the motif. A hand in a gutter, clutching a bottle of cheap brandy, suggests a life of defeat and despondency. The hand with the bottle is, in literary terminology, a *metonymy* of the life it suggests.

Another example: In the opening shot of Fassbinder's *The Marriage of Maria Braun*, we see a portrait of Hitler, which is immediately smashed by a grenade, leaving a gaping hole in a brick wall through which we see a man and a woman, the man wearing an officer's uniform and the woman in a bridal dress. They turn from the smashed window and answer, one after the other, "Yes." It is one of the most masterly film openings ever made; we know we are in Germany, we know the Third Reich is nearing its end, we know an officer of the Wermacht is getting married. And it is all told in two or three seconds! It is done by way of carefully chosen metonymies that *suggest* the whole situation of which they are part.

NARRATIVE RICHNESS: THE USE OF METAPHOR

In literature, the use of *figurative discourse* marks the style of many accomplished writers. Words are given meanings that are entirely different from their everyday usage. When two distinctly different subjects or entities are joined together verbally in such a way that the attributes of one blend with and enrich the other, thereby creating new meanings, we are dealing with _metaphor._ For instance, the expression "the river of life" uses the image of the river to suggest a certain quality of life. "The long arm of the law" suggests the difficulty of escaping justice.

Unlike metonymy, which is a concrete, physical part of the whole it depicts, a metaphoric image in film suggests meanings that are only abstractly connected to the object itself. It works by way of similarity. For instance, an hourglass may be used to suggest a certain quality of life: At first we hardly notice the sand running through it, then, as it nears the end, the sand _appears_ to run faster and faster. The hourglass is not a _part_ of life, it is only a very evocative _image_ of it. The qualities of the hourglass are carried over to suggest _similar_ qualities of human life.

Example: In Pakula's _Klute,_ Jane Fonda, who plays a fashionable call girl, finds herself desperately in need of someone to talk to. She seeks the company of an old man who has, on earlier occasions, given her money just to be in her company. Arriving at his office, she finds that he has gone, leaving her an envelope containing money. As she looks in despair at the money, she is surrounded by the headless display dummies of the office.

The dummies are perfectly natural in their place. The way the filmmaker uses them at this moment, however, suggests certain likenesses to Fonda's _situation._ She is no less an object than they are.

It should be noted that metaphors in film work best when, as in the example above, they also have a perfectly realistic function. Heavy symbolism, divorced from reality, easily feels empty and pretentious.

6
FILM SPACE

A number of film stories have been undermined by the filmmaker's having insufficient control over the *screen geography*. It is difficult to be committed to the action if you cannot find your way around. In this way, a good screenplay can become a confused story.

Reality as portrayed on the Plane of Events is *endless and three-dimensional*. The audience, however, sees this reality on a *two-dimensional, rectangular screen*.

The actual space must be re-created and formed to give the spectator the impression of an unbroken and *continuous* physical space. The three dimensions of reality must be "translated" by way of a certain set of rules into the two-dimensional *space relationships* of the screen.

This is done by providing the spectator with the necessary *references*, i.e., a milieu is established in which there is a *left* and a *right*, for example, and these relationships remain constant until others are established.

It is easy for the filmmaker to be deceived by his own knowledge of what the locations of the film actually look like. The audience, however, knows nothing outside of what is shown or suggested by the images. This is both the strength and the weakness of film. In a confident manipulation of space, the filmmaker has one of his most effective tools.

Below, by means of examples, we shall consider screen geography and spatial relations, bearing in mind their dramatic consequences in both cases.

Screen Geography

EXAMPLE: *Dallas*, Episode 13

Series such as *Dallas* or *Dynasty* use a narrative technique that is so obvious that anyone in any part of the world is able to follow the story. The viewer must swiftly and efficiently be told where he is.

Episode 13 of *Dallas* opens with an exterior shot (fig. 1) where a large sign informs us that we are outside a police station. Even the arrow directs our attention toward the inside.

The dialogue belonging to the second shot (establishing the scene inside) actually begins during the first shot and is at the same volume as in shot 2. (In other words, the two shots are linked together by this overlap in dialogue.) There is, therefore, not the slightest doubt that we are inside the police station. The first thing we notice is Bobby, who is talking at the moment of the cut. He is also placed at the point indicated by the arrow in the first shot, he is facing the camera, is the best-lit person in the scene, and is wearing a bright blue suit, which stands out in the picture. He is sitting between the two policemen, facing his interrogator. The other interrogator walks past him and sits in a high position on the edge of the desk to the left of the screen. In this situation, Bobby is in a position of inferiority.

EXAMPLE: *Dynasty*, Episode 8

1a

1b

2

3

Episode 8 of *Dynasty* opens with a shot of a fountain outside a skyscraper (fig. 1a). The camera tilts up toward the top of the building (fig. 1b). The tilt does not quite come to a halt before the shot dissolves to an interior scene where Carrington is seated at a desk (fig. 2). Thus we know that he is in an office high up in the building.

Track in toward Carrington, who asks his secretary to call his wife. Cut to an exterior shot of an opulent house (fig. 3). The camera zooms in on one of the windows while, at the same time, we hear a telephone ringing. Cut to a wedding photograph of Carrington and Krystle (fig. 4a). The camera pans around to the left, past a telephone that is still ringing, and stops on Krystle, who is lying on the bed (fig.4b) without reacting. Zoom in on her face. The dialogue, the phone ringing, and the camera movements join the two scenes together to form an organic piece of action that leaves no room for ambiguity.

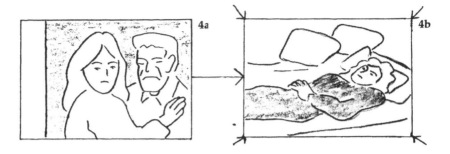

EXAMPLE: Carné's *Le Jour se lève*

We find a more gentle and sensuous way of being led into a setting in the opening shots of *Le Jour se lève*. While shot 1a is fading in, we hear the sound of hooves. From a high angle we look down on a roadway crossed by tramlines. A horse with a rider and another horse drawing a cart come into the shot. The camera tilts, following their movements into the picture, and we see a square with buildings on all sides. Because of its height and particular shape, one of these buildings stands out from the rest (fig. 1b). The sharp sound of the horse's hooves bridges the cut to shot 2a, where rider and horses come into view from the right while we glimpse the foot of the building on the left. At first the camera pans with the rider to the left,

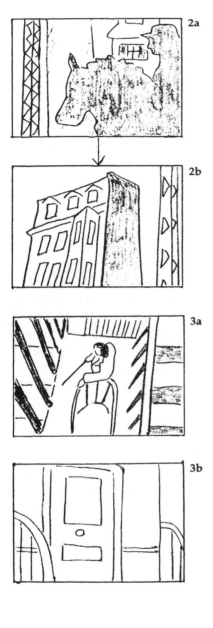

2a

2b

3a

3b

then leaves him and tilts up, following the front of the building and stopping at the top (fig. 2b). Dissolve to a high-angle shot of a spiral staircase (fig. 3a).

A man carrying a white stick comes into the shot and the camera tilts upward again, leaving the man, passes one floor, and stops at a door on the floor above (fig. 3b). Before the tilt comes to a halt we can already hear the sound of two men arguing loudly. The quarrel continues till we hear a shot, the door opens, and a well-dressed, middle-aged man staggers out with his hands pressed to his stomach. He falls forward and begins to tumble down the stairs. What is notable about Carne's opening is that he presents all of the essential details in a completely unobtrusive way. The *horse* catches our attention and leads us into the picture, where we immediately notice the boarding house. In the next shot the horse motivates a camera movement (panning), which subtly changes to a tilt, and we get a closer view of the boarding-house. A second *interior* tilt is helped by the movements of the blind man. So, three consecutive tilts are instigated by a moving subject on the Plane of Events, pullingus, as it were, into the physical environment.

Notice that we leave the horse and rider in shot 2a. The fact that the camera tilts up the front of the building rather than following them is an indirect indication that they are not important—the film is not going to be about them. Their job is taken over by the blind man, who leads the camera upward once more. Before the camera has time to stop a third time, something new has begun, which takes a dramatic turn at the moment of the gunshot. We do not for one moment wonder where we are—we are on the top floor of the easily recognizable boardinghouse.

EXAMPLE: Pontecorvo's *The Battle of Algiers*

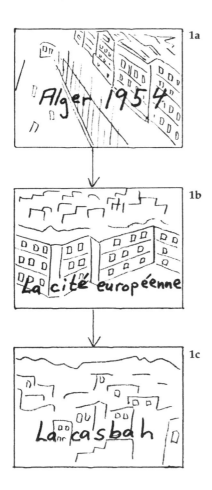

In *The Battle of Algiers*, one single camera movement gives us the complete picture of the geographical rapport between Frenchmen and Arabs, the two antagonists of the drama. The film opens with a big overview of a street in a big city; a superimposed text tells us that this is Algiers in 1954.

The camera begins to pan slowly to the right, and when the high-rise buildings that flank the broad boulevards dominate the picture, a new text tells us that this is the European quarter. The camera pans farther to the right, leaves the high-rise buildings, and zooms in on the cluster of chalk-white houses that are draped over the hillside in the background. The text informs us that this is the Casbah. An important precondition for the conflict in the film has thus been presented—the French stick to the center of the city while the Arabs live in the surrounding hillsides. The panning is an effective way of illustrating the geographical rapport and also indicates the great architectural differences between the two quarters. This is all the information we need in order to know our way about later in the film.

EXAMPLE: Truffaut's *The Bride Wore Black*

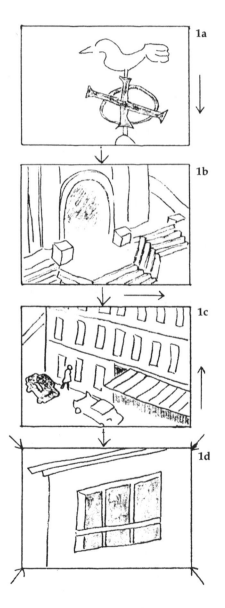

One of the most central flashbacks in *The Bride Wore Black* opens with a close-up of a church spire (fig. 1a). The camera tilts down the front of the church at the same time as the picture becomes wider by zooming out. By the steps of the church, the tilt becomes a pan to the right (fig. 1b), over an open square to the front of a building on the other side (fig. 1c). Here the movement changes to a tilt up the front of this building and comes to a halt at the top floor. We zoom in on the window to the left (fig. 1d). Throughout the camera movement we have heard a variation of Mendelssohn's Wedding March. Immediately before the cut to shot 2 (interior), the music changes and adopts a somber tone. In shot 2 we see a group of men sitting around a table.

The important thing for the events that are about to take place is that we know

exactly where the five men are in relation to the church (the spire, the clock, the steps). All through the sequence we are reminded of the fact that the church is on the left and the apartment is on the right. We are aware of this even in the close-ups. This scene is an example of very thorough and clear scene setting, which enables us to concentrate wholly on what is dramatically important.

EXAMPLE: Kubrick's *2001: A Space Odyssey*

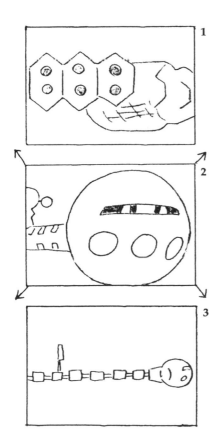

In the second part of *2001*, where we meet the spaceship on the way to Jupiter, some intimation must be made of the endlessness of space and the monotony of life there. In shot 1 the ship glides slowly to the right, away from the camera. In shot 2 the camera virtually travels with the spaceship, which approaches us at an angle. Shot 3 shows the ship at an angle, sideways on, as it glides in its entire, enormous length, past the camera. 4a-4d show us a crewman running around the edge (which is actually the "floor") of the spinning space capsule, his head always toward the center of

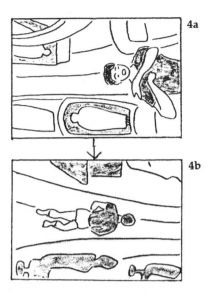

4a

4b

the vessel. He runs almost two complete laps in the eternal circle while the camera pans with him to show the whole scene.

In shot 5, the camera tracks after him, and in shot 6 we see him in a low shot with the camera backing away in front of him, travelling at the same speed as the man. As always, Kubrick uses a wide-angle lens, which makes the camera movements seem exaggerated and gives the setting a dominating, almost life-like stamp.

Mankind becomes small and insignificant.

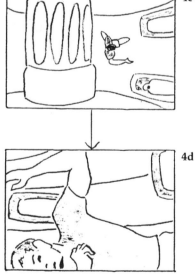

4c

4d

5

6

EXAMPLE: Scott's *Alien*

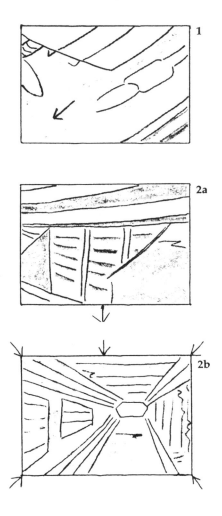

Alien, where an alien creature terrorizes the crew of a spaceship, is a science-fiction film of a completely different sort than *2001*. While we have a more or less complete overview of the setting in *2001*, in *Alien* it is essential that we do *not* have such an overview.

In shot 1, the spaceship glides slowly over us to the accompaniment of indistinct mechanical noises and music. Cut to the first interior shot (2a), which is a sideways tracking shot along cramped spaces full of cryptic instruments and dim shadows and corners. The movement comes to a stop in 2b as the camera tracks inward along a narrow corridor that has a light at the end. In shot 3 the camera continues to track in a complex pattern, going close in on objects that we cannot quite distinguish. Shot 4 is the first one where the camera is stationary. This is followed by several static shots of ill-defined objects, and then the instruments begin to come alive and the computer screens light up. The crew members are being roused from their sleep.

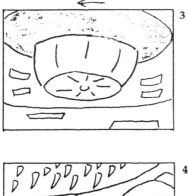

It is dramatically essential that, while the scene is being set, we have *no* chance to get a complete view of the setting or to identify the "futuristic" objects. There are shadows, nooks, and crannies everywhere, and it is here that the deadly creature will come to hide—a creature that changes appearance and that we do not see completely until the end of the film. In other words, a feeling of insecurity is established that is purely physical and geographical.

EXAMPLE: Hitchcock's *North by Northwest*

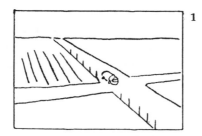

As an introduction to the famous "plane sequence" in *North by Northwest*, we get a very high overview of the bus stop where Cary Grant alights (fig. 1). The bus drives off and Grant is seen as a mere speck in the great expanse of wilderness. The shot lasts all of 53 seconds.

Shot 2 is a long-shot of Grant watching the bus as it disappears toward the horizon (fig. 3). In shot 4 we have another medium shot of Grant, who turns away in the opposite direction. All there is in that direction are

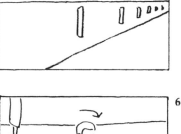

the posts by the side of the road (fig. 5). Grant peers ahead (fig. 6) only to confirm that there is nothing there either (fig. 7). Finally he turns completely round (fig. 8) and sees that there is nothing in that direction but a small track that does not seem to go anywhere (fig. 9).

Hitchcock takes great pains here to tell us that there is nowhere to hide or take shelter. This is very important later when the plane attacks.

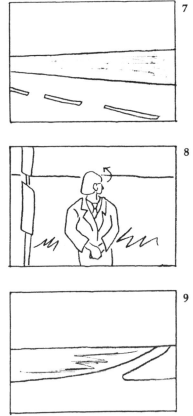

EXAMPLE: Kubrick's *The Shining*

In *The Shining* the three members of the family are shown through a gigantic hotel in which they will be working in the mountains. Here a thorough scene-setting is made easy since it consists of the new arrivals being shown around. After the usual establishing shot of the hotel (fig. 1) we are shown the reception area in a long tracking shot (fig. 2), which stops at an armchair where Nicholson is sitting, waiting. The scene dissolves to the Colorado Hall and a new introductory tracking shot (fig. 3). After an intermezzo where the son sees the two murdered girls, we come back to the guided tour, which has now reached the staff quarters (fig. 9). The family apartment, including the son's bedroom, is shown (fig. 10).

In the following shots, we are taken on a giddy tour of the kitchen, refrigerator cupboard, storerooms, etc. spiced with small incidents that forebode terrible things. In this way Kubrick underscores the enormous size of the hotel and at the same time gives the different places a life-like quality by track-

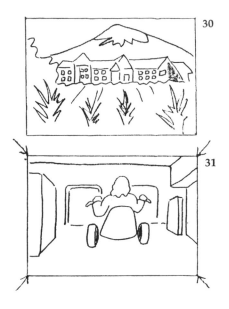

30

31

ing in big, wide shots that make us _feel_ the distortions in perspective. The evil is in the very walls. Time and again in the film, Kubrick re-establishes the scene to show the passage of time (shot 30). In shot 31 he gives us what is perhaps the most suggestive tracking shot in the whole film, where the son rides through the hotel in his pedal-car. We now know the places pretty well and are prepared to see something horrible. Terror may lurk around any of the corners the boy turns.

Spacial Relations

EXAMPLE: _Dallas_, Episode 13

1
2

G. J.   B. J.   B

The first scene in Episode 13 of _Dallas_ is a conversation between Bobby and two police officers in a police station. Let us call the police officers "Black Jacket" (sitting down) and "Grey Jacket" (half standing).

2
9
15

B. J.

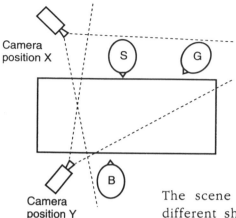

Camera position X

Camera position Y

B

3
5
10
12
14
16
18

G. J.

4
8
11
13
17

B. J.

G. J.

6
19

The scene consists of six different shot types, all of which are interchanged. For simplicity's sake, we can say that all of the shots were taken from two camera positions (although certain adjustments are made for each shot): *camera position X* for shot 1 (establishing shot), shot 3 (C.U. Bobby) and shot 7 (M.S.—medium shot—Bobby), and *camera position Y* for shot 2 (C.U. Black Jacket), shot 4 (C.U. Grey Jacket), and shot 6 (two-shot of Black Jacket and Grey Jacket).

The first thing we notice is that the scene both begins and ends with the establishing shot. It *opens* in order to set the scene and *closes* in order to give a summary—a common way of coming into and leaving a scene. (When the establishing shot is repeated at the end—and not until then—a certain distance is created. We know, without needing to

think, that the scene is finished.) Shot 2 is a close-up of Black Jacket, shot 3 a close-up of Bobby, and shot 4 a close-up of Grey Jacket (who, with his eyes, acts as an intermediary between Black Jacket and Bobby). In order not to have *too* many close-ups, thereby spoiling their effect, the film cuts on two occasions to a two-shot of Black Jacket and Grey Jacket (shot 6 and 19) and once to a medium shot of Bobby (shot 7). The shot that occurs most often is the close-up of Bobby (7 times)—he is the dramatic focal point in the scene.

Scenes in series such as *Dallas* usually have a construction that adheres strictly to the rules. The traditional shot sizes alternate and great care is taken to maintain the established spatial relations. The audience must always know exactly who is where and who is looking at whom. Here we have a confrontation between Bobby and the two policemen. The policemen are placed on the *left* and Bobby on the *right*. The *line of interest* (or 180° axis) here is a straight line between Bobby and Black Jacket, and the camera follows the rules by remaining on one side of this line. Bobby looks obliquely to the left and the others look obliquely to the right. When Grey Jacket shifts his gaze from right to left, we know that he is looking from Bobby across to Black Jacket—it fits in with his position between them.

(Grey Jacket here poses a potential problem. Probably he could *not* have been shot in close-up from camera position Y if this shot had been cut in immediately after the establishing shot where he is *to the left of both the others*. In order to shift his gaze from Bobby to Black Jacket, he would have had to shift from oblique right *away* from the camera to oblique right *toward* the camera. But since shots 2 and 3 come in between, shot 4 can be inserted without causing problems.)

A scene such as this one is well worth studying. It provides a simple, easily understood key to the narrative logic of most TV series made for the worldwide market. The narrative language is extremely clear and unambiguous. Without thinking, the audience is able to follow the dra-matic turn of events.

EXAMPLE: *Dynasty*, **Episode 8**

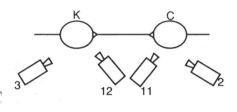

A scene from *Dynasty* can be used to illustrate what some people call the five basic camera positions during an exchange of dialogue between two people.

First, the scene is *established* (shot 1) in a shot of both people together, at approximately right angles to them. Then we have *over-the-shoulder shots*, with one person facing the camera and the other in the foreground, mostly outside the frame (shots 2 and 3). Finally there are the *close-ups* (shots 11 and 12) when the dialogue becomes heated.

In this scene between Krystle and Claudia, the rules have been strictly adhered to. It is a long and harrowing confrontation between them and this is evident from the close-ups that fill the second half of the scene.

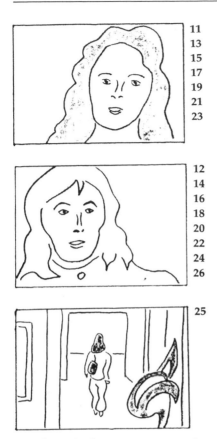

11
13
15
17
19
21
23

12
14
16
18
20
22
24
26

25

This dramatic build-up distributes the dramatic weight more or less evenly between the two. Shot 3 is a _reverse shot_ of shot 2 (and vice versa) while shot 12 is a reverse shot of shot 11 (and vice versa). This means that both people appear to each other in the same shot size and from corresponding camera angles. Reverse shots must not be confused with _point-of-view_ shots (subjective shots), where the camera is placed so that it "sees" from the person's point of view, i.e., through that person's eyes. A look at the illustrations will tell us that this is not the case for shots and reverse shots (the camera is on one side of the line of interest between them).

There is, however, one point-of-view shot in the scene. In shot 23, Claudia turns angrily on her heels and goes away. Cut to Krystle (shot 24—reverse shot), who glares after her. In shot 25 we see Claudia through Krystle's eyes (she is going away from the camera)—a point-of-view shot. The last shot (26) is another close-up of Krystle. By finishing with the close-up of Krystle, the dramatic weight is placed on her. It is through _her_ eyes that we see in the end and her reaction carries the dramatic interest.

If we make use of point-of-view shots, the pattern _objective shot - point-of-view shot - objective shot_ should be followed (unless there are valid reasons for not obeying the rule). The logic is as follows: objective shot 1—the person who sees; point-of-view shot—what he/she sees; objective shot 2—his/her reaction to what he/she sees. The rule is therefore justified dramatically, according to the maxim that _nothing has meaning in drama until someone reacts to it_. (If we do not cut back to the person who sees, the point-of-view shot is pointless!)

EXAMPLE: Truffaut's *The Bride Wore Black*

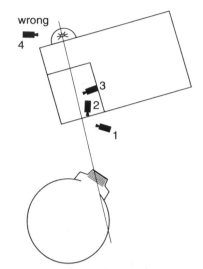

As we saw in the earlier example from this scene, Truffaut has created a clear relationship between the apartment and the church steps, with the church on the left and the apartment on the right. If we draw a line through the church steps and the apartment, this relationship is maintained as long as the camera remains to the right of this line of interest (as shown in the illustration above). Trauffaut does this right through as far as shot 4. In this shot, Truffaut crosses the line and makes it seem as though the five men run down the spiral staircase at the *front* of the house, in full view of the church steps. Is this a *deliberate* crossing of the line?

Film theorists disagree on this. Some say that by crossing the line, Truffaut creates a stronger feeling of anxiety in the audience and the breach is therefore justified (it has, in our terminology, a dramatic function). Others see the breach as a plain example of non-function; the shot was presumably made by a second unit, working on a completely different location at a different time. They were simply not aware of the geography of the original scene.

EXAMPLE: Hitchcock's _The Birds_

One of the classic scenes in _The Birds_ achieves its effect by means of a sure control of screen geography.

Melanie has gone to the school to warn the children of a possible bird attack. While the children are singing an apparently endless song, Melanie goes out onto the steps outside the school to wait for the end of the lesson (shot 1a). The camera pans with her as she begins to walk along the path to the left, past a large junglegym (shot 1b). A little farther along, she comes to a bench and sits down (shot 1c). The next shot (2) is composed so that we see Melanie on the bench in the foreground, slightly to the right of the picture. Behind her, farther to the right, we glimpse the school building. In the background, to Melanie's left, the junglegym is clearly visible. A black bird flies into the picture and lands on the junglegym. Melanie does not see it.

This is the _only_ shot in the scene where we see Melanie, the school, and the jungle-gym with the birds _in the same shot._ The effect of what follows depends wholly on our having a clear picture of the screen geography in our

minds—i.e., as established in shot 2: the junglegym *slightly to the left* behind Melanie and the school *slightly to the right* behind her.

In shot 3 there is a slight change of angle so that we get a better view of the school in the background but do not see the junglegym. Melanie lights a cigarette. In shot 4 we see *only* the junglegym, and now there are three birds perching on it.

Shot 5 is similar to the previous shot of Melanie but a little closer in. She is smoking distractedly.

Shot 6 shows another bird coming to perch on the junglegym.

Shot 7 is like shot 5. Melanie turns her head to the *right* and looks behind her toward the school.

In shot 8 there are eight birds on the junglegym and a ninth lands on it.

Shot 9 is an even closer shot of Melanie; twice she turns impatiently and looks at the school, then her attention is caught by something in the air above her.

Shot 10 (a point-of-view shot for Melanie) shows a black bird flying towards the right.

In shot 11 (a close-up) Melanie follows the bird with

9

her eyes (eye movements from right to left).

In shot 12 the bird continues on its flight and lands on the junglegym (12b). We see that the frame is crowded with black birds.

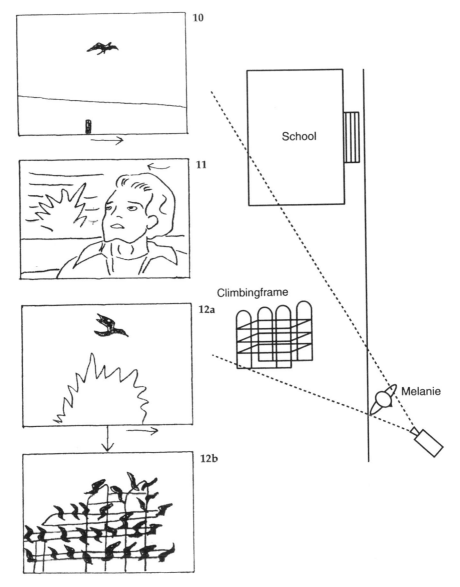

We can ask what would have happened if shot 2 had been omitted, leaving only the establishing shot where Melanie walks from the steps, past the junglegym to the bench. Probably this would have caused so much confusion as to ruin the whole dramatic effect. In shot 1a-1c *both* the junglegym *and* the school are located to the right of Melanie. When she turns in the close-ups and looks to the right behind her, we would assume that she *sees* the birds on the junglegym. What makes her react would then be *the last bird*, and why should she react to that one and not to the others? Her behavior would be confusing.

Since shot 2 shows the junglegym slightly to the *left* of Melanie, no such confusion arises. When she turns her head, we know that she can *only* see the school and we squirm in our seats, willing her to turn her head a little more so she can see the birds as well.

EXAMPLE: Hitchcock's *North by Northwest*

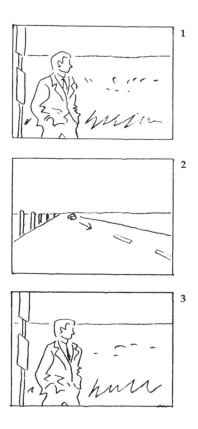

In *North by Northwest*, Cary Grant is standing at a bus stop in the middle of nowhere, waiting for someone he believes he is supposed to meet. At first he thinks that this person will come by car, so he devotes his (and our) attention to all the cars that go by. In shot 1, he hears a car approaching from the *right*, so he looks to the right. Shot 2 shows the car approaching from the *left*, moving toward the right. Shot 3: Grant looks right, toward the car. Shot 4: The car approaches, moving from left to right. Shot 5: Grant's eyes follow the car from right to *left* as we hear it pass. In shot 6, we see the car going away toward the *right* of the frame.

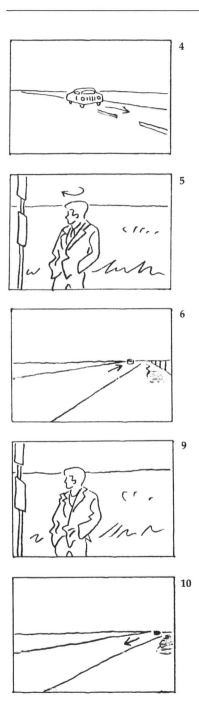

According to the fundamental rule, when a person sees an object to his right in one shot, in the following shot the object must maintain the same relationship with respect to the person. In other words, it must be on the right or come into view *from* the right. In this example from Hitchcock, this rule is consistently broken. Grant looks to his right and the car approaches from the left. The car disappears away to the right and Grant stares after it to the left.

The same thing happens in shots 9-16, though in this case the car is travelling in the opposite direction. The reason for this ostensible breach of the rule is that Hitchcock constantly inserts *point-of-view shots* of what Grant sees. Apart from the shots of Grant, we see *everything* through his eyes, including the passing traffic. Here Hitchcock deliberately crosses a line: the line of movement of the cars.

As can be seen from the illustration, here we are dealing with *two lines*.

One is the *line of interest* between Grant and the object of his attention and the other is the *line of movement* of the car itself. In order not

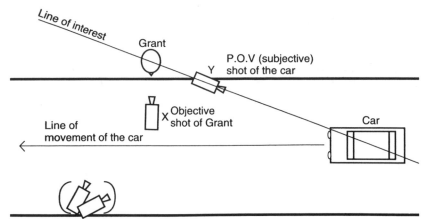

Line of interest

Grant

P.O.V (subjective)
shot of the car

Y

X Objective
shot of Grant

Car

Line of
movement of the car

Required camera position
if left-right relationship
is to be maintained
(no subjective shots)

11

12

to break the right-left relationship, the camera must be placed *on the same side of both lines* in all the shots where the moving object appears (as shown in brackets in the illustration). From all these camera positions, Grant looks to the right and the car comes *from* the right, as we expect it to.

If, however, we cross the car's line of movement, as we must do if we use point-of-view shots, the car in the shot will be moving in the "wrong" direction; Grant looks to the right and the car comes from the left. This has a disorienting effect and is probably deliberate on Hitchcock's part. A feeling of psychological

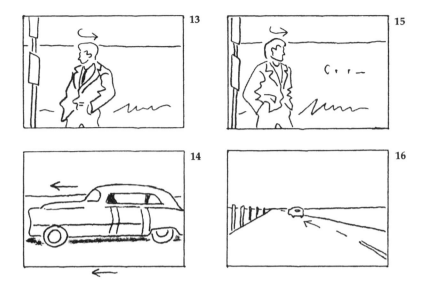

insecurity is created. (Things are coming from unexpected directions and we know that danger lurks somewhere. Where?) Moreover, Hitchcock works according to the pattern objective shot - point-of-view shot - objective shot, and he sticks to this narrative logic (which is the principal tool of the suspense film) rather than submitting to the right-left rule. It is the _dramatic_ logic that determines which breaches of the rules are permissible in which situations.

7

TIME

Time is a very flexible category in film and TV. Only rarely does *film time* (i.e., the length of time we, the audience, spend watching the film—the "viewing time") coincide with the *story time* (the length of time—real or imaginary—required for the events in the film to realistically take place). This happens only in exceptional and strongly motivated cases such as Zinnemann's *High Noon*.

It is nearly always necessary to *shorten time* in some way, either *visibly or invisibly.* We find invisible cuts in every scene where non-essential time is made to "disappear" by means of cuts that are not noticed. For example, we may have an interior scene with a man in the foreground and a telephone on a table in the background, some twenty feet away from him. The phone rings, the man turns and begins to run toward it. He has only had time to run a yard or two when we cut to a close-up of the telephone. A tenth of a second later the man's hand appears in the shot and picks up the phone. He cannot possibly have reached the telephone in such a short time, but we do not notice this "cheating" because we are concentrated on the objective of his running, namely the phone. Psychologically we want him to get there as soon as possible.

Visible time cuts occur when we *emphasize* the passage of time, e.g., from day to night or from summer to winter. But even here, the cuts can be made smooth and elegant, e.g., by cutting from the dinner table to the pile of dirty dishes in the kitchen. This narrative device is often referred to as "elliptical" it is understood tacitly that a certain length of time has elapsed.

Lengthening time is less common but can sometimes be both dramatically and lyrically justified, e.g., in the last moment of suspense or in a love scene where time stands still.

The elastic nature of time in film even allows us to *mix different planes of time*. Alf Sjöberg's *Miss Julie* gives one of the most subtle examples of free time treatment in the history of the cinema (see below).

Real Time and Film Time
(Story Time and Narrative Time)

EXAMPLE: Antonioni's _The Passenger_

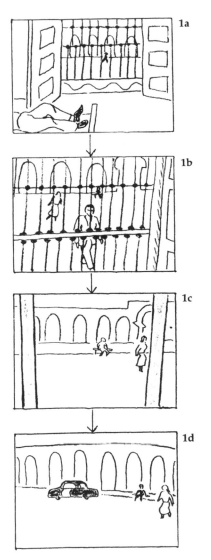

The penultimate scene in *The Passenger* is a seven-minute take without cuts. Naturally, in a case like this, story time (real time) and narrative time (film time) are the same, but this does not mean that the scene must appear static. On the contrary, the fact that one does not cut can, as in this case, become part of the basic suspense in the film.

As the scene opens (shot 1a), we see Jack Nicholson lying on a bed in a Spanish hotel room. Through the bars on the window, we look out over an open square with a bullring on the other side. While the camera creeps slowly toward the window, a number of more or less significant things happen outside. Maria Schneider, who has just left Nicholson, paces doubtfully to and fro, children play, a car draws up and disgorges two men, whom we recognize as agents for an

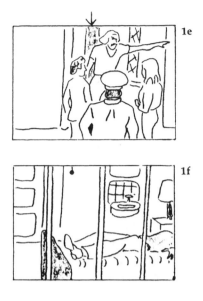

African government. One of them walks by the window and the other looks in (shot 1b), tries to divert Schneider's attention, and drives off. Just after this we hear police sirens (shot 1c) and the camera tracks *through* the bars of the window (shot 1d), alights on a second police car, which Nicholson's wife and some policemen get out of, follows them to the hotel entrance, where the owner directs them to Nicholson's room (shot 1e). Finally the camera comes to rest in front of Nicholson's barred window and we see that he is lying motionless on the bed. The policemen, the wife, and Schneider come into the room and see that Nicholson is dead (shot 1f).

The consistent limitation of perspective means that we are deprived of the best overview of events. The murder—if murder it is—takes place outside our field of vision. Instead, we observe a series of events that may or may not be significant. We are made to use our own imagination to make connections and draw conclusions from a series of *incomplete* clues. We are made to look more closely and interpret the truth that lies under the surface in much the same way as we would have to do if we were real spectators at the scene. When used in this way, the "real time" sequence serves to stimulate the imagination of the viewer.

EXAMPLE: Widerberg's The Baby Carriage

The Baby Carriage, Widerberg's impressionistic-realistic first film, presents examples of what we may call _elliptical_ time precis. By this we mean that major events are abbreviated in the film to become a few shots that _imply_ the whole event.

In one scene, the central character, Britt, is sitting at home in her flat, looking discontentedly at her boring, drab lampshade (shot 1). Cut to a close-up of Britt (shot 2). Cut to a medium shot of Britt's parents in their home, sitting on the sofa watching television (shot 3a). The camera pans to the left until we see through the door into the next room, where Britt is standing on the table taking down the elegant, shining chandelier (shot 3b). Cut to an interior shot of a tram, where Britt stands holding the chandelier (shot 4). Cut to a close-up of Britt walking in the dark with the chandelier (shot 5). Cut to Britt's flat, where the chandelier now hangs. Britt turns on the light and looks contentedly at the chandelier (shot 6).

Widerberg sees no reason for showing the whole trip to

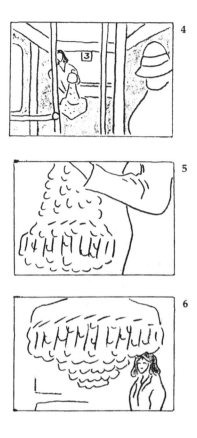

and from the parent's home. He only shows enough for the story to hang together.

Although it is rather brief, the close-up of Britt (shot 2) gives us the impression that she sits thinking for a long time. We expect that she will take some action now. The subsequent change of place is marked by carefully showing the parents on the sofa. Since change of place often also means change in time, we find it easy to accept the fact that Britt is there in the background. Britt's return journey home is marked by two shots (both very brief), one on the tram and the other of Britt walking in the dark. If shots are used that only show a person moving from one place to another, they must be used to say something—in this case they have a slightly comic effect (it is awkward to travel on public transport carrying a chandelier). Then all we have to do is switch on the light and the chandelier is in place.

(Notice that the comic surprise effect in shot 3b would have been lost completely if Widerberg had chosen to show us Britt's journey *from her home to her parents.*)

EXAMPLE: Truffaut's *Jules et Jim*

1   Narrator: 1912. Jules, a stranger in Paris, asked Jim to take him to the Art School Ball. Jim got the tickets and costumes.

2   It was when Jules chose a slave costume that Jim's friendship for Jules was born. Jules was calm and his eyes were full of humor and tenderness.

3   They met every day.

4   Each learned the other's language. They showed each other their poems and translated them together. Neither cared much for money and neither of them had ever had such an attentive listener.

5   Jules had no woman.

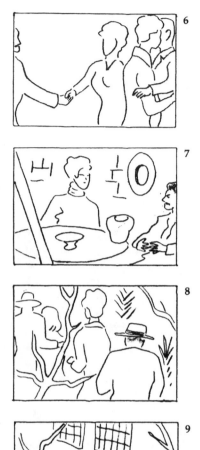

6 Jim had several. He introduced Jules to a young woman, who was a musician.

7 Jules was in love for a week and so was she.

8 Then there was a woman who haunted the cafés until six in the morning.

9 Then a blonde widow. The three of them went out together.

10 She was bewildered by Jules.

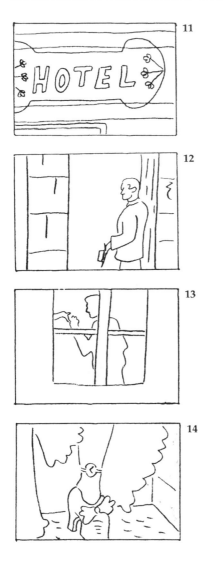

11   In the end Jules—

12   —resorted to contact with professional women—

13   —but without finding—

14   —any satisfaction.

The sequence illustrated above is the first one after the opening credits in Truffaut's *Jules et Jim*. Here the continuity in time is wholly a function of the narrator's voice. The shots are simply impressionistic illustrations—as it were, moving snapshots in an album. We could say that the visuals are lyrically independent; there is no coherent continuity between them (apart from the last four, which deal with the *same* episode). Time is just not relevant in this opening sequence of shots or at least it has no other function than that of establishing a sort of musical rhythm. Real time has been dissolved in the *time of the spoken narrative*. Even shots 11 to 14, which show Jules' visit to the "hotel," simply allude to the visit. Still pictures could have done the job just as well.

Invisible Compression of Time

EXAMPLE: Polanski's *Knife in the Water*

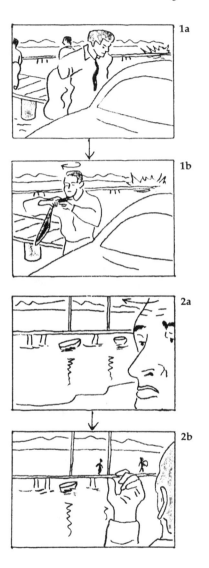

In *Knife in the Water*, Polanski makes cuts in time that are virtually imperceptible unless one is looking for them. In the foreground of shot 1a, we see the husband, who is taking off his jacket. In the background, his wife and a student they have picked up walk out along a jetty and disappear from view. The man turns toward the left while he loosens his tie (1b). During this movement, Polanski cuts to shot 2a, a close-up of the man with a more distant part of the jetty in the background. The movement of the man's head in 1b is continued in shot 2a. A second or so later we see his wife and the student come into view, far out on the jetty (shot 2b). They simply *cannot* have walked so far in such a short time, but Polanski makes the *time cut* on the wife and the student by *continuity cutting* on the man.

This is an unusually skillful example of how an interval of time can be compressed so that "dead" time can be eliminated in an imperceptible way (thus leaving more time for what is dramatically important).

EXAMPLE: Polanski's _Cul-de-Sac_

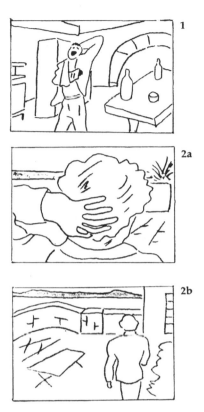

In _Cul-de-Sac_ the "gangster" wakes up one morning in the palace kitchen. He stretches and yawns as he holds the back of his neck with his left hand (shot 1). In the middle of the yawn Polanski cuts to a close-up of the man from behind (shot 2a); the movement of his hand continues from shot 1. As the man begins to walk, the camera pans with him to the right and reveals that he is out on the terrace. The continuity cut on the hand movement, combined with the close-up, masks the change of scene and obviates the need to actually show the man's movement from interior to exterior in a completely unobtrusive way.

EXAMPLE: Truffaut's _The Bride Wore Black_

One of the transitions in _The Bride Wore Black_ shows how carefully each shot and each cut must be planned when we want to foreshorten time in a way that the audience will not notice.

Jeanne Moreau has just pushed one of her husband's murderers from a hotel balcony. In shot 1 we see the man lying on the pavement far below where she stands. Shot 2: Objective shot of Moreau. Cut to a close-up of her feet as she walks briskly across the balcony. They turn and go out of the shot, which for a moment remains on the feet of a man wearing black shoes (shot 3). Brief shot (4) of Moreau's shawl, which is hanging on a parasol outside the balcony rails. Cut to the receptionist, who is talking on the telephone on the ground floor. He does not see Moreau run by behind him (shot 5).

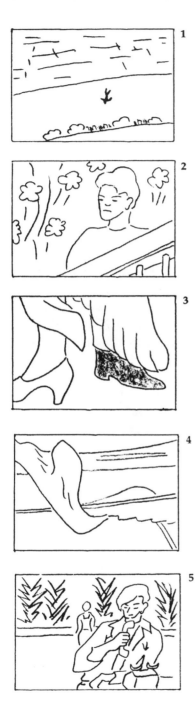

The shot of the shawl here enables Truffaut to eliminate Moreau's journey down to the ground floor, a journey that is dramatically superfluous. In shot 6 Moreau continues running away from the hotel.

All these shots have been accompanied only by dramatic music. At the cut to shot 7 the music changes to a sort of interlude music played on a guitar. The wind picks up Moreau's shawl and carries it away, high over the town. The camera follows the shawl until, a white speck, it floats down toward the palm trees in the distance (shot 7b). A few seconds before the next cut, the music stops and we hear the sound of a jet plane.

Cut to a worm's-eye view of the shawl, which has become caught in a tree (8a). The plane flies over and the camera follows it, zooming in at the same time (8b). New "expectant" music begins as we cut to Moreau sitting by a window on the plane (shot 9). Zoom in on Moreau, who is writing in a notebook, which she closes and then looks out through the window. Cut to a high aerial view of mountainous terrain (10). Dissolve to an-

other aerial shot of a cluster of houses in a valley between the mountains (11). Cut to a low shot of houses and telegraph poles (12a). Pan to an open window, where a man appears (12b). He looks up to the sky (at the plane?). The next sequence is under way.

The long pursuit of the shawl as it floats over the town gives the impression of a long passage of time, though in reality it is only forty seconds. In that time, Moreau cannot have got very far. But we can hear the plane *before* the shawl lands, and after the zoom-in on the plane we suddenly find ourselves with Moreau on the plane! And after two very brief aerial shots, we have reached our destination— the mountain village where the next victim lives. The man looks up at the plane, and a few seconds later Moreau appears in the hotel corridor!

All this is done not in accordance with real time but in accordance with *narrative logic.* As an audience, we want to be assisted in as smooth a way as possible as we progress from one dramatic situation to another. As long as the dramatic logic is

maintained, we accept without question this kind of drastic compression of time. We are completely wrapped up in the subjective time of the story and give no thought to the unrealism of the time-compressing narrative devices.

EXAMPLE: Pontecorvo's *The Battle of Algiers*

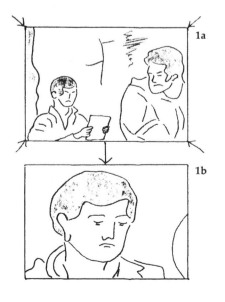

Boy: An Arab café in the Rue Randon in the Casbah. The owner's name is Magherb. He is a police informer.

Boy: Every day at five o'clock a cop arrives—

2

Boy: —he stays a few minutes— exchanges a few words, pretends to drink a cup of coffee—and then leaves. You will kill the cop.
Ali: Not Magherb?
Boy: No!
Ali: All right.
Boy: You can't go wrong.

3

Boy: Near the café a young girl stands holding a basket.

4

Boy: Go with her and follow the cop.
When the moment comes—

5

Boy: —she'll give you the gun.

6

Boy: All you have to do is shoot him—in the back and quickly.

Despite its apparent documentary tone, Pontecorvo's *The Battle of Algiers* is carefully planned to the last detail. The example above shows how easily the director takes us from one day to the next. In shot 1a the boy begins to read out the orders from the rebel forces to Ali-la-Pointe at the same time we zoom in on the boy. As he begins to talk about the café owner's daily meeting with the cop (1b), we cut to a shot of *what he is talking about* (shot 2). *This shot is not yet placed in any time;* it is simply a shot of something that takes place every day. However, in the next shot (3), while the boy is talking about the girl with the basket, we *see* Ali, who is looking questioningly at the girl. Then we have three shots (4, 5, and 6) of what the boy is reading out; Ali and the girl together follow the policeman. In shot 6, when the boy has finished reading, the street sounds are turned up to normal volume and we are "really" at the scene of the next day's attack.

Via the temporally neutral shot 2, Pontecorvo crosses over visually to the described events of the following day long before the boy has finished reading. Ali is already doing (on the screen) what the boy says *he is going to do* the next day—"tomorrow" in sound is "today" in image. Doing it this way is far more elegant than having the boy read the letter and then dissolving to the following day (a transition in time we would *notice*). Here we do not really know how it is that we suddenly find ourselves at the scene of the attack on the day of the attack—the transition is masked by the identity between what is said and what is seen.

Visible Compression of Time

EXAMPLE: De Sica's *Miracle in Milan*

Vittorio De Sica's neo-realistic fairytale *Miracle in Milan* begins with the words "Once upon a time . . ." printed over the first shot (1). A pleasant and happy old lady finds a baby in her garden. She takes the baby into the house and lays it on her bed (shot 8). Dissolve to a big close-up of

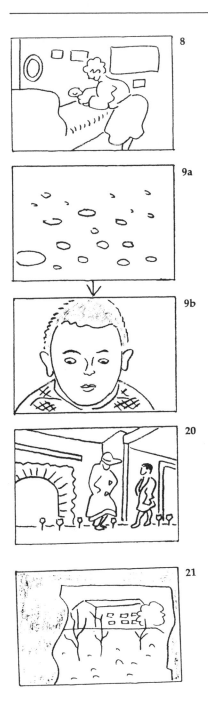

some milk boiling over (9a). The camera tilts up and stops on a boy of seven or eight who is staring, fascinated at the milk (9b). The old lady comes in and instead of being angry she thinks of a game to play with the milk (shot 20). Cut to a shot through the window and we see it is a dull, grey day (shot 21). The next shot shows us that it is the boy who is standing looking through the window; he turns and walks toward the bed where the old lady now lies (22). Two solemn-looking men arrive, send the boy out, and take the lady's pulse. She looks uncomprehendingly up at them (shot 34). Direct cut to an exterior shot, where we see a horse-drawn hearse; the boy is the only one who follows it (shot 35).

When the journey through the town is over, we see two men in formal dress, who take the boy through the large front door of an orphanage (shot 56). A fade-out to black is immediately followed by a fade-in to the same picture as the previous one; two men come out with a younger man between them (shot 57). The boy has grown up. He takes leave of his guardians and goes out alone into the world.

In the true spirit of the fairy tale De Sica, in a few brief and well-chosen episodes, tells us all we need to know about the boy's background and growth. In some instances the "jumps" in time are considerable. The old lady hardly has time to look after the baby before it becomes a young boy (with the boiling milk—shot 9a—as a connecting shot). There is another connecting shot (21) and the old lady is ill in bed. We do not need to see her death; the cut from taking her pulse to the shot of the hearse tells us unmistakably what has happened. The most daring time cut comes perhaps in shots 56 and 57. The boy is taken into the orphanage, and in an almost identical shot we see him come out again—an adult.

The lapses in time here are emphasized; we are supposed to notice them. De Sica uses the well-tried *dissolve* to indicate the passage of time (from shot 8 to shot 9a and from 20 to 21). However, from 56 to 57 he needs to fade out and in since the two pictures are the same.

The treatment of time is *elliptical*; a long period of time is hinted at by means of a few key events that *imply* the passage of time.

EXAMPLE: Welles' *Citizen Kane*

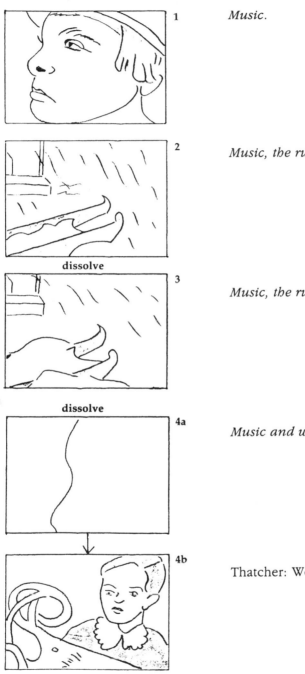

1   *Music.*

2   *Music, the rustle of wind.*

dissolve

3   *Music, the rustle of wind.*

dissolve

4a   *Music and wind fade away.*

4b   Thatcher: Well, Charles—

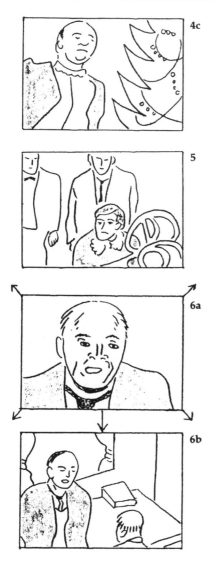

4c Thatcher: Merry Christmas!

5 Kane: Merry Christmas.

6a Thatcher: And a happy New Year.

6b Thatcher: In closing, may I again remind you that your 25th birthday, which is now approaching, marks your complete independence from the firm of Thatcher & Co., as well as the assumption of your full responsibility for the world's sixth largest private fortune. Have you got that?

In this example from *Citizen Kane*, Orson Welles bridges over twenty years in a few seconds. Shot 1 is from the childhood of Kane, the central character; he has just learned that the banker, Thatcher, is taking him east, away from his parents' home. Charles Kane stares threateningly up at Thatcher. Dissolve to Kane's sled, which lies abandoned in the snow (shot 2). Dissolve once more to the sled, which is almost covered by snow (shot 3). (This way of showing that time has gone by is very effective; we dissolve to the *same* picture where certain *changes* in the shot indicate the passage of time.) Dissolve to a completely white shot, crossed by a cord (4a). Dissolving from white to white means that we hardly notice it. The cord is taken away, some paper is drawn back, and we see (4b) that Kane is holding a sled in his hand (a completely different type of sled from the one previously abandoned). Tilt up to Thatcher, who is wishing him Merry Christmas. Kane returns his wishes (shot 5) in a very virulent way. Cut to Thatcher, who says ". . . and a Happy New Year" (6a). The camera tracks back and we see that Thatcher is dictating a letter—a message to Kane about his approaching 25th birthday and the fact that he can now assume responsibility for his fortune.

These drastic transitions are softened by the technique of cutting on similarities and associations (from white snow to white paper, from sled to sled) and by creating an illusory continuity in the dialogue ("Merry Christmas"—shot 5, "and a Happy New Year"—shot 6a—almost twenty years later). These fluid transitions create flow and continuity *at the same time* as they give a clear indication of the passage of time. Note that shot 6a of Thatcher *could* show his reaction to Kane in shot 5. The shot is temporally neutral until the camera moves back to reveal the enormous time lapse. It is this *illusory* continuity that holds the scenes together.

EXAMPLE: Kubrick's *2001: A Space Odyssey*

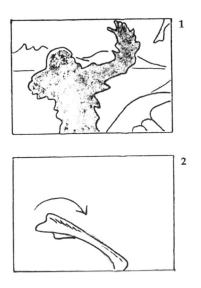

It is hard to imagine a more radical cut in time than the one Kubrick makes in *2001*. The ape from the "dawn of man" hurls his newly-discovered weapon to the skies (shot 1). The camera follows the bone as it sails through the air (shot 2). Cut to a satellite carrying nuclear weapons as it glides in space (shot 3). The entire history of the human race has gone in one single cut.

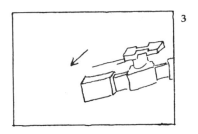

Here too (as in *Miracle in Milan* and *Citizen Kane*) the leap in time works by the use of *analogy*. The piece of bone—a symbol both of progress and of destruction—is linked to the armed satellite. The cut thus becomes a sad comment on human development.

EXAMPLE: Welles' *Citizen Kane*

Leyland: Well, after the first couple of months, she and Charley didn't see much of each other—except at breakfast. It was a marriage—just like any other marriage.

Shot 2-8: We know from the dialogue that Kane and Emily have spent the night at six different parties. Emily asks why he has to go straight to the newspaper office, and Kane replies that she should never have married a newspaper man. However, he decides to put his appointments off until lunch.

Emily: It's late.

Kane (with an expectant grin): It's early!

Shots 10-13: Emily chides Kane for making her wait for hours the night before. Kane tries—somewhat impatient-ly—to calm her down by as-suring her that her only rival is the newspaper.

Shots 15-22: Emily com-plains about
Kane's attacks on the Presi-dent in his newspaper.
Emily: He happens to be the President, Charles, not you.
Kane: That's a mistake that will be corrected one of these days.

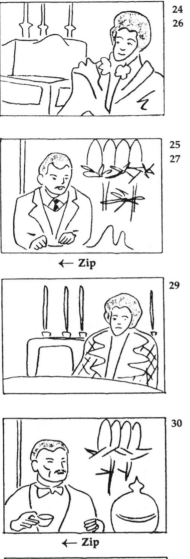

24
26

Shots 24-27: Emily asks Kane to urge Bernstein (Kane's editor) to stop sending vulgar presents to their son. Kane refuses.

25
27

Emily: Really, Charles—

← Zip

29

Emily: —people will think...

30

Kane: What I tell them to think!

← Zip

32

Silence.

33a *Silence.*

33b *Silence.*

34

Reporter: Wasn't he ever in love with her?

In the above sequence from *Citizen Kane,* Orson Welles compresses a long-lasting marriage into a little over two minutes of film time. Kane's old friend, Leyland, is talking to the reporter about Kane's life with Emily: "It was a marriage just like any other marriage." Here we dissolve to a large establishing shot of the room where Kane and Emily are having breakfast. The camera tracks in for a closer shot of them as they sit beside each other on one side of the table. Welles then cuts to medium shots of each in turn (shot-and-reverse-shot technique). The atmosphere is intimate and charged with eroticism.

The switches in time in this sequence are marked by slow dissolves superimposed on a zip pan of the interior. After each pan we notice that Kane and Emily have changed clothes, and there have also been changes to some details in the decor. In the second breakfast scene (shots 10-13), Kane is sitting farther from Emily and he is also smoking a pipe.

Each time the camera swish-pans (shots 9, 14, 23, 28, and 31), the mood becomes more implacable. The scenes also tend to become shorter; the penultimate breakfast scene consists of two brief shots (29 and 30). In shot 33 Welles tracks back to a long shot where each of them is sitting reading a newspaper (Emily has the *rival* paper) on opposite sides of the table. The warmth and intimacy of the opening scene have now become hostile silence.

The principle behind Welles' cuts in time is, to vary *some* of the elements in a situation that is otherwise repeated. Each little difference says something about how the relationship has changed and is, therefore, an indirect indication of the passage of time.

Lengthening Time

EXAMPLE: Forman's *One Flew Over the Cuckoo's Nest*

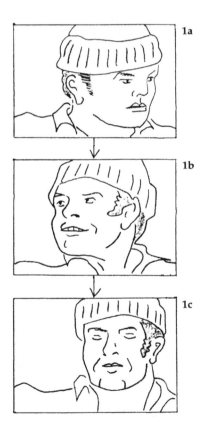

1a

1b

1c

The length of time one shot can last before we cut to another depends first of all on the amount of information contained in the shot. A mass of details, movement of subject, camera movement, the steady unfolding of events, and so forth can make it possible to work with long takes without making the time seem long. The sense of time is also influenced by the type of shot, action, and rhythm of cutting that immediately *precede* the shot in question. In this way it is possible to manipulate the *subjective* sense of time to a considerable extent. A good example of this is to be found in Milos Forman's *One Flew Over the Cuckoo's Nest.*

At the end of a rather chaotic sequence where the patients have been celebrating Christmas in the middle of the night, McMurphy, who is on the verge of running away, stands beside the window to wait for his girlfriend. The camera holds him in a close-up that lasts a little over one minute.

Subjectively it feels much longer because the information contained in the shot remains almost constant. MacMurphy has a thoughtful expression on his face (1a), he turns once or twice toward the window with a smile on his lips (1b), then he closes his eyes (1c). In the next shot the sun is shining through the window.

We expect a narrative to keep us steadily supplied with new information once we have "registered" the information that has already been presented. If this does *not* happen, we become immediately aware of the *time*. It is as if everything stands still. This can be used in a creative way, to *suggest* a long period of waiting (as in the example above).

EXAMPLE: Truffaut's *The Bride Wore Black*

In *The Bride Wore Black*, immediately after the fatal shot has been fired toward the church steps, Truffaut emphasizes the action with an audacious narrative device. The *same* action (in real time) is shown *three* times. In shot 1 the bald man lifts the rifle *completely out of shot*.

Shot 2 is a point-of-view shot of the same action seen through the telescope sight, which tilts from the wounded bridegroom up toward the sky. In shot 3, which has been taken from outside the window, we see once again how the bald-headed man lifts the rifle in through the window.

However, the three shots *feel* like one and the same action. The fact that we are not aware of any feeling of lack of realism is due to the sudden dramatic weight of the situation where the thrice-repeated movement serves as emphasis in rather the same way as we underline a passage in a book. The effect is also partly masked because the logical sequence objective shot - point-of-view shot - objective shot is maintained. The music also helps; the same interrupted snatch of Mendelssohn's Wedding March is repeated three times.

Mixed Time Levels

EXAMPLE: Resnais' *Hiroshima mon Amour*

Flashbacks—shots from a previous episode in the life of a person— are nowadays accepted items in the filmmaker's repertoire of devices. But few have been able to mix past and present with such mastery as Alain Resnais in *Hiroshima mon Amour.* The film shows how an episode in the heroine's past intrudes on her consciousness and gradually overwhelms her. In the lyrical-dramatic climax of the film, she walks through the deserted streets of Hiroshima at night while scenes of the past assail her constantly. Resnais visualizes this by tracking alternately along the streets of Hiroshima and those of the girl's home town, Nevers, in France.

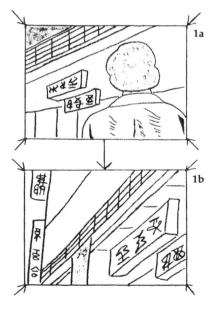

In shot 1a the camera tracks, following Emmanuelle Riva from a fairly low angle, passes her, and glides over the bright neon shop signs (1b). Cut to a tracking shot along the front of another row of buildings (shot 2). Cut to a tracking shot at the same speed to a sign on a wall saying "Place de la Republique" (shot 3). Cut to a tracking shot on a Japanese sign (4). Track to the right, past typical French buildings (5). Track to the left past Japanese shop signs (6). Continued tracking at exactly the same speed through a French townscape (7). Track to the right across a French square

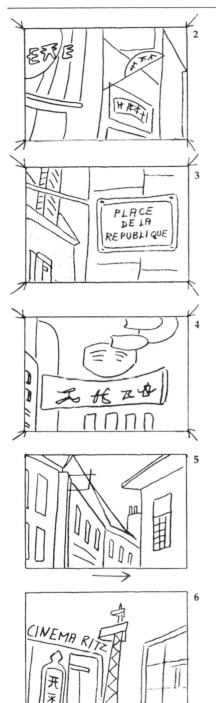

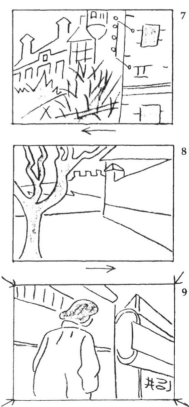

(8). In shot 9 we follow Riva once again as she wanders through Hiroshima. Other shots that are put together in the same way then follow.

One of the factors that determine the success of this is, naturally, the fact that Resnais, through his narrative style, has already established the hold that the past has over Riva. The sequence constitutes an organic entity by making play of *similarities* and *contrasts*. The same almost dreamily sensual camera movements are there both in Hiroshima and in Nevers, as is the somber piano music and Riva's poetic inner monologue. However, the photographic character of the images is different: the Japanese shots accentuate the contrast between light and dark, while the shots in Nevers (taken by another photographer) have a soft, lyrical quality of grey—the color of nostalgia.

EXAMPLE: Antonioni's *The Passenger*

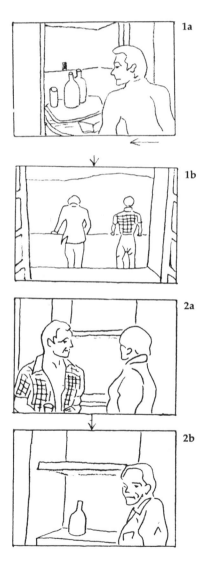

An unusual way of mixing the present with the past is found in *The Passenger.* Jack Nicholson sits, stripped to the waist, listening to a taped conversation between himself and a hotel guest who has recently died (1a). The camera pans left and stops at an open window. Robertson (the dead man) comes into view on the veranda outside. Nicholson follows and stands beside him, only now he is wearing a checked shirt and his hair is well-groomed (1b). The conversation goes on, but now both men are talking in sync. Cut to a door, which opens and the same two men enter. Nicholson gets a glass (shot 2a) and goes out of shot. Robertson turns toward him and continues talking (2b). A few seconds later the camera pans right and stops on Nicholson, who is once again sitting shirtless and perspiring, listening to the taped conversation (2c).

Here, then, we have two different planes of time represented *in the same take*. It is impossible to say at *exactly* which point the present becomes the past—they flow into each other in one psychologically uninterrupted time.

EXAMPLE: Angelopoulos' *The Travelling Players*

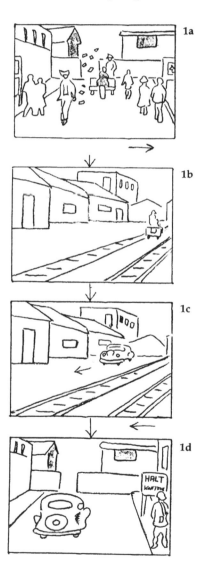

Megaphone voice: If we don't want to see our streets sullied by the hammer and sickle, if we don't want another Red December, we must rally round the Marshal. Your vote will make Sunday, 16th December an historic day, a victory for the nation.

Megaphone voice: So vote for Marchal Papagos. A vote for him is a vote for the only candidate beloved throughout the land, the man who led our armed forces to victory over the Communist uprising of 1947-49. The Marshal guarantees peace, well-being, law and order.

Silence.
Sound of car approaching.

Sound of car approaching.

Angelopoulos' great historical film *The Travelling Players* shifts constantly among different points in time in the period it covers. One of his aims in doing this is to show how certain political and social patterns are *repeated* under various guises in different historical conditions. We are constantly being torn from one reference point in time and set down in another where, however, we rediscover the same social contrasts, the same arguments, the same lies, and the same strategies.

In the above example, a three-wheeler drives through the streets of a small town in Greece with one officer throwing out leaflets while another shouts into a megaphone (shot 1a). The walls of the houses are covered by posters that show the Fascist leader whom the soldiers support. The vehicle turns up another street (shot 1b) and disappears from view. The voice from the megaphone grows weaker, and after a few moments of silence, a car comes along from the direction in which the three-wheeler disappeared (1c). The camera follows it back to the opening shot, where the only person in sight is now a guard in German uniform (1d). The posters and leaflets are gone and in their place we see a large sign bearing the legend "HALT. KONTROLLE."

In one and the same take we have been transported from 1952 back to the days of World War II.

EXAMPLE: Sjöberg's Miss Julie (I)

1   Jean: But she is handsome—strong—

Jean: —such shoulders and—etcetera
Kristin: Oh come on, that's enough.
I've heard what Viola says, who has dressed her.
Jean: Ssh! Viola! And haven't I been out riding with her?
Kristin: Mmm. Then you must have seen something worth seeing.
Jean: I'll tell you what—do you know what I saw the other day down by Lover's Point?

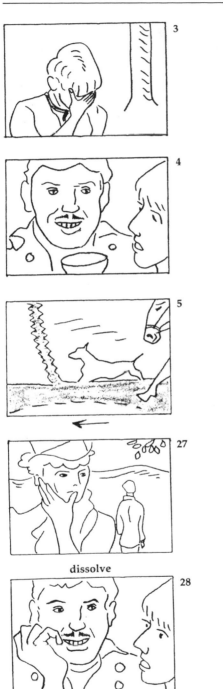

3

Jean: Ha, ha, ha!

4

Kristin: What did you see?
Jean: Well, it was the very
day Diana was unfaithful.
Miss Julie wanted to go
down to the lake to see the
waterlilies, and her fiancé
and I went with her.

5

Music.

27

Music.

dissolve

28

Jean: And that was the end
of the engagement.
Kristin: Oh Lord! And there
she sits now.
Jean: Yes, there she sits
now.

29   *Midsummer music begins.*

In *Miss Julie,* Alf Sjöberg achieves a degree of flexibility and control over the treatment of time that is seldom seen. The film shows how it is possible to take any sort of liberty, provided one has mastered the art of *building up* to the desired effect.

Sjöberg does not *begin* with the most complex and blatant manipulations of time; he inserts them stealthily and gradually. He does this by allowing the pictures to submit to and support the *narrative logic.* It is the narrative logic and not the chronology of events that determines where and to what he can cut.

The above illustrations show how Sjöberg establishes a narrative logic that he later develops into complex manipulations of time. The main principle is that he consistently *cuts in the direction of our interest.* Each shot can be said to contain a main thought that justifies the placing of that shot in the whole, and this thought must guide our interest. Each series of shots represents a *train of thought,* and this train of thought captures and nurtures our interest. The above example may serve as an illustration of this principle.

Miss Julie has left in a carriage to join her father, who is celebrating Midsummer at another house. On the way, she stops by a lake and drifts into thought (shot 1). While the picture remains on Julie, on the soundtrack we hear Jean begin to talk about her and then we cut to Jean and Kristin in the kitchen of the manor house (2). When Jean begins to recount what he saw at Lover's Point, there is a cut to a *reaction shot* of Julie—as if she could hear what he is saying (3). But she is merely at the same place (Lover's Point) and remembers the episode he is relating (i.e., it is their *thoughts* that coincide). Here Sjöberg begins to build up his narrative logic: *we see on the screen an event that is being related.* In shot 3 there is no shift in time yet, but Sjöberg is easily able to introduce it in shot 5 once Jean has begun to tell what really happened at Lover's Point. In the following shots up to shot 27, the events that

Jean refers to are allowed to speak for themselves, without any commentary from Jean on the soundtrack. The action itself *assumes* the narrative function. Only after the dissolve back to the kitchen in shot 28 does Jean pick up the thread again, and the whole first flashback then appears as something he has recounted. At the line "There she sits now" we cut to Julie (shot 29), who is now back *at the same point in time* as Jean and Kristin. She raises her head as if to shrug off the memory of what has just been said. Then she turns her horse around and goes back toward the manor house.

Two different places and two different times. But every shot fits in with the others like cogs in a well-oiled machine.

EXAMPLE: Sjöberg's _Miss Julie_ (II)

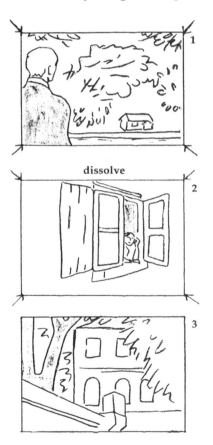

Jean: Can you see the other side of the lake—the laborer's cottage in the fields? That was my home. There were eight of us children and a pig. No tree grew there, but from the window I could see the wall of the Count's grounds—

Jean: —with the apple trees on the other side. It was a Garden of Eden—

Jean: —and a host of evil angels watched it.

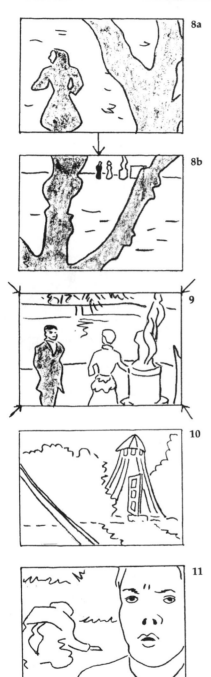

8a

Dramatic music.

8b

Music finishes.

9

Jean: You feel contempt for me, don't you?
Julie: Contempt? But surely all boys steal apples.
Jean: Another time I went into the garden with my mother to weed the onion beds and the garden paths. Over there where the Jasmine blooms, there's a Turkish Pavilion.

10

Jean: The door had been left open that day.

11

Jean: I'd never seen such a lovely building before. My mother wasn't looking so I plucked up courage—

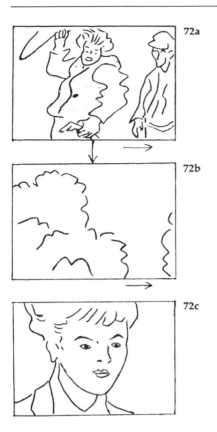

72a   _Sound of blows and cries._

72b   _The sound of blows contin-_
ues, becomes gradually
weaker as the midsummer
music is turned carefully up.

72c   _Midsummer music._

In this example Sjöberg begins to build up a special narrative technique in order to connect the various planes of time in which the film moves. Jean is telling Julie about his childhood. In shot 1 they walk toward a little lake, and on the other side of it we glimpse a house where Jean says he grew up. Slow zoom-in toward the house, which dissolves into a much closer zoom-in on the window of the house where we see Jean as a boy (shot 2). Jean's voice continues to tell of how, from the window, he could see the walls of the Count's grounds, and the apple trees and the next shot (3) shows us this. With every cut—and with the help of zooming— we are led deeper into (we might say backward into) Jean's story. At first, the two of them see the cottage in the present, then the zoom-ins and the dissolve lead us gently over into the past till, in the end, the Count's orchard is what Jean sees _as a boy._

In the following shots we see how the boy is chased from the garden by the housekeeper. In shot 8a she stops beside a tree and looks around before going out of shot to the right. The camera tilts up until in the background we see Jean and Julie in conversation by the lake. Here past and present have been united in one uninterrupted take. (The transition is helped by the fact that the music stops at the same time as the camera tilts up on Julie and Jean.) Shot 9 is a conventional continuity cut from 8b; Jean continues his story while the camera tracks in for a closer view of the two. When he starts to talk about the Turkish Pavilion, he looks up toward something that is out of shot. Cut to the Turkish Pavilion (shot 10). In shot 11, the boy Jean sticks his head up in the foreground and looks with wide, admiring eyes in the same direction as Jean the adult. This is an interesting example of how the logic in the sequence objective shot - point-of-view shot - objective shot can be used to unite two separate planes in time. Shot 10 (the point-of-view shot) is neutral in regard to time; it would look identical whether seen in the past or in the present. By means of this *neutral* point-of-view shot, objective shot 1 (the present) can be linked to objective shot 2 (the past), and we pass over immediately to action in the past.

The sequence ends with Jean being caught by the Count's servant and beaten by his father (shot 72a). The camera begins to pan past the silent onlookers until it leaves the group completely. It glides past the trees in the park, comes down past a lilac bush, and comes to rest on Miss Julie—back in the present once more. Only then is the sound of the beating turned completely down. Once again the fusion of past and present is only a narrative device, but a highly effective one. We feel that the past is *present* just as it is for the person telling the story.

EXAMPLE: Sjöberg's *Miss Julie* (III)

1

Julie: My mother over there came from a very simple home. She was brought up on—

2a

2b

100

105a

105b

Julie: —the new ideas regarding women's liberty and so on. So my father said when he proposed to her:

Count: Ha, ha! No, she said, she wouldn't be my wife but she wouldn't mind being my mistress. Ha, ha.

Music.

Music.

Music finishes.

In this example, we see once again how Sjöberg uses a shot that is *neutral* as far as time is concerned to join the present to the past. Julie is talking about her mother, whose portrait hangs on the wall. Jean looks up toward it (shot 1). Cut to the portrait (2a). The camera tracks in for a close-up of the portrait's face only to pull back the next moment and change angle so that we suddenly see the Count, who stands holding the portrait up with his hand. In shot 2a the portrait is a point-of-view shot in the present while, during the camera movement, it becomes an objective shot in the past. There is also continuity between Julie's lines and the Count's. Julie (during the point-of-view shot): "So my father said when he proposed to her." The count (in the subsequent "objective" part of the shot): "Ha, ha! No, she said, she wouldn't be my wife . . ." In other words he picks up where Julie leaves off so that his words go together organically with hers.

Later in the sequence, Sjöberg uses the same technique to return to the present. The Count looks up anxiously at the portraits on the wall (shot 100). We see five different ancestral portraits. On the last of these (105a), the camera tilts down and we see Jean in the mirror, looking upward—in the present.

We soon become so used to these transitions that Sjöberg later dispenses with the neutral point-of-view shot and pans directly from Jean and Julie to the Count. It has become an agreed *convention* for the treatment of time.

EXAMPLE: Sjöberg's *Miss Julie* (IV)

 1

Music.

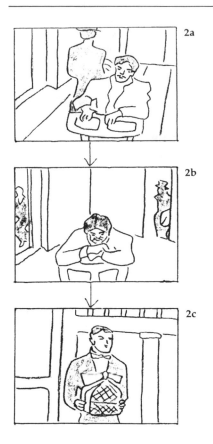

2a

Julie: She taught me to hate and suspect men.

2b

Jean: So one fine day you went and got engaged to the Commissioner of Police.

2c

Police Commissioner: Just a little Christmas present.

The treatment of time in _Miss Julie_ reaches it greatest degree of complexity in the example above. Past and present flow completely together. The adult Julie sits in the foreground while the mother with the infant Julie in her arms passes by in the background (shot 1). They pass Jean in shot 2a and go toward the door on the right in the background. _Before_ they go out of the shot, we see some-one _stand up_ in the mirror to the left (2b). The camera pans right and picks out the Police Commissioner who, in a medium shot, goes to give Julie the Christmas present.

Three different time-levels involved at one point here. Jean (in the present) in the foreground, the mother and Julie (the infant) in the background to the right, and the Police Commissioner (some months earlier) reflected in the mirror to the left.

This would never work unless it had been thoroughly prepared during the course of the film. Sjöberg utilizes narrative devices that lead us, step by step, away from conventional realism. In the end, he can do pretty much what he likes: He shows on the screen what Julie *conjectures (imaginary time)*; at one point we see both her and what she is thinking at the same time.

The only important factor is that the *narrative logic* guides the narrative tools. If the formal creation is an organic expression of the narrative, there is, in principle, no rule that cannot be ignored. *From its own logic* the narrative creates its own rules.

8

EDITING

Editing is not simply a matter of joining two strips of film together in such a way that the rules of continuity are obeyed (though this, naturally, is one of the fundamentals that must be adhered to). *Where*, *how*, and *when* cuts are made depend, in the first place, on the *style* of the film as a whole. A cut that is right in one situation may be quite wrong in another.

Cuts can be made to involve the spectator in the action or they can be made in such a way that he is kept at a distance from it. We can look for meanings *in* what we film or we can use what we film to *create* meanings.

In the final analysis, the editing style boils down to a question of how the filmmaker *relates* to the world he is portraying. To take two extremes: On the one hand is the filmmaker who is not interested in the segment of reality at which he aims his camera; he only uses *pieces* of this raw material to construct meanings that are not to be found in the material itself but which are *created* by the way in which he puts the pieces together. In this case, the real world per se has no value but serves as a subordinate means to the primary end, which is the narrative or the abstract argument. On the other hand, we have the filmmaker who examines a segment of reality that is more or less unfamiliar to him and that he wants to capture in as genuine and unmanipulated (at least by him) a condition as possible. In this case the question of whether one should cut time, space, and action into pieces becomes decisive. This applies to fact as well as fiction.

We shall illustrate this with some examples.

EXAMPLE: Hitchcock's *Psycho*

In *Psycho*, Hitchcock gives us numerous examples of the style by which his films are able to enthrall the spectator in the grip of suspense. The illustrations here are taken from the build-up to the climax of the film: Lila is on the way up to the great gloomy house where we know (but she does not) that people have been murdered. Hitchcock switches constantly between objective shots and point-of-view shots. As we come closer in on Lila with each cut, she comes nearer the house (shots 1-5). After she opens the door and steps into the completely silent house, Hitchcock cuts to a shot of her friend Sam and Bates, the owner of the motel (shot 14). The whole exchange of lines between them is shot from this angle; there is no dividing into shot and reverse-shot on them *because our attention is not on them*, it is on Lila. The drawn-out long shot and the dialogue create a point of tension. Now we are jumping in our seats with impatience to get back to Lila. Close-ups on Sam and Bates would immediately have given *them* dramatic weight, which would have broken our concentration on

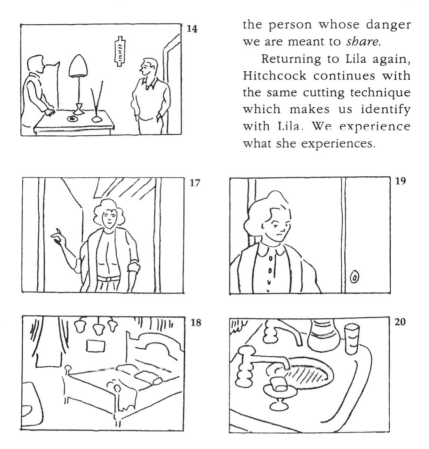

the person whose danger we are meant to *share*.

Returning to Lila again, Hitchcock continues with the same cutting technique which makes us identify with Lila. We experience what she experiences.

EXAMPLE: Resnais' *Hiroshima mon Amour*

In *Hiroshima mon Amour*, Resnais works with a style based on the logic of subjective association. Impressions of the present are mixed with pictorial recollections of the past until, in the end, the two blend together.

If this style is to work, the subjective experience of reality must be established as the guiding factor in the ordering of shots.

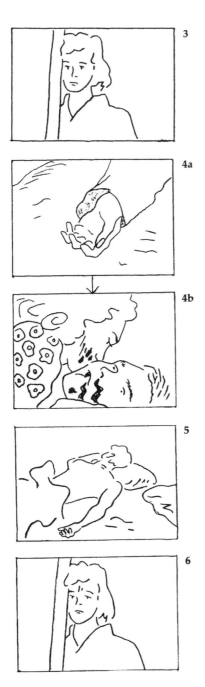

The scene illustrated shows how the first brief flashback occurs to the film's central character, Emmanuelle Riva.

From a veranda with a view over Hiroshima, she walks back toward the room where her Japanese lover is still sleeping. She stops in the doorway and looks at him tenderly (shot 1). Cut to a point-of-view shot of her lover on the bed; his outstretched hand stirs (2). Back again to a closer objective shot of Riva, who suddenly looks troubled (3).

Cut to a close-up of a completely different hand (4a); the camera tilts quickly upward and we catch a glimpse of a woman who presses her cheek against the bloodied face of a man (4b). Direct cut to the lover on the bed again (5)—a shot that is identical to shot 2. Back to a shot of Riva (6), whose face registers great pain.

Shots 1-3 lead us in the conventional way into Riva's experience (objective shot - point-of-view shot - objective shot) so we expect shot 4 to be a point-of-view shot. However, it is a subjective *flashback* that is linked to the other shots by *association* (the lover's hand—bleeding man's hand). With shot 5 (point-of-view, present) we are back with Riva again.

A cutting style that follows the _laws of memory_ has been introduced. Continuity in space and time has been replaced by a _montage of association_ that follows the subjective whims of memory

EXAMPLE: Eisenstein's _Que Viva Mexico!_

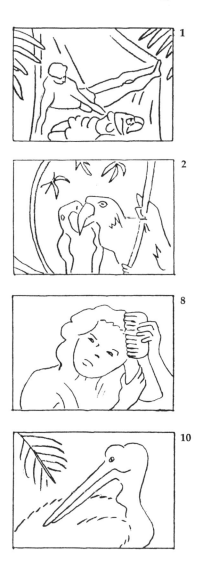

In the classic Russian montage, the meaning of each shot was of itself not important. By _connecting_ the shots (this is what montage means), meanings were created that did not exist in the segment of reality that had been filmed. So there was never a question of "letting reality speak for itself" but rather of the director's using parts of what he had filmed in order to make his own _comments_. No attempt was made, therefore, to make "invisible" continuity cuts. What was required was what Eisenstein called a "collision" between shots that would bring about the intended meanings. The takes were short and the camera usually static. In this example from _Que Viva Mexico!_ we can see something of this method at work. The film consists largely of a mosaic of well-composed images. In shot 1 we look down upon two lovers in a hammock. Cut to a pair

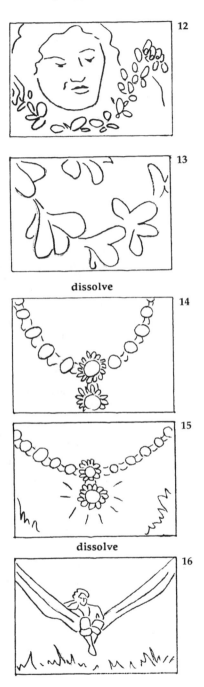

12

13

dissolve

14

15

dissolve

16

of parrots that "kiss" each other (shot 2). A few shots later, we see another woman who is combing her hair (shot 8). "She is proud of her beauty, Conception," says the commentator. After a new close-up of Conception, we cut to a pelican, which is "combing" its plumage (10).

Conception holds up a garland of flowers (12). Cut to a big close-up of flowers (13). Commentator: "A gold chain, that's what she is dreaming about." Dissolve to a gold chain around Conception's neck (14 and 15). While we are dissolving to a similarly composed shot of a young man in a hammock, the commentator says: "That's what all the girls in Tehuantepac dream about. It is their dowry, the guarantee of happiness."

If we consider each shot by itself, its informative value (though not its poetic value) is minimal. Shots 1-10 talk of the universal coquetry of love; the cuts to the shots of the birds link love and beauty to nature itself. Nature and cultural tradition are again united when the garland of flowers becomes a gold necklace that gives rise to a visualized expectation of happiness (the young man in the hammock).

Close-ups abound in this cutting style and this is not surprising. The close-up is an *extract* of a whole physical context and as such can be *abstracted* completely from the context and used as an element in the construction of a new context of meaning.

EXAMPLE: Bunuel's *Viridiana*

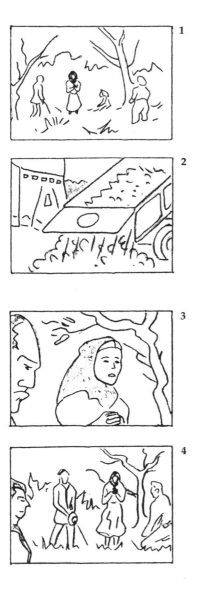

In *Viridiana* we find a realistically based cross-cutting, which, nonetheless, creates meanings that cannot be gleaned from the mere sum of the individual shots.

At the same time as the land owner is organizing the work in his grounds, Viridiana, the former nun, gathers her poor disciples together in prayer (shot 1). Cut to a lorry, which empties its load of sand at the manor house (2). Back to Viridiana and her monotonous droning (3 and 4). Cut to a saw, which is sawing up a log (5). And so it goes on: Shots of Viridiana and her poor band are cut against shots of various building activities at the manor house. Viridiana concludes her prayer, and the beggars disperse in a long shot (which is identical with shot 1). Taken separately, the two parallel events deal with prayer and work. Edited together by Bunuel in this way, they form a contrast that is a *thematic conflict*: spiritual versus materi-

al, passive versus active, tradition versus renewal.

Unlike Eisenstein, Bunuel creates thematic contrasts with pictures of things happening there and then. Eisenstein created meaning with pictures that could have been taken from anywhere (the birds, for example, were presumably photographed in a different place alto-gether). For Eisenstein, the symbolic expression is all that matters, whereas for Bunuel the symbolism must be extracted from the real world in which his characters move. Eisenstein looks for a free symbolic pictorial language that is unhampered by any ties to realism; Bunuel tries to create a realism that is rich in symbolic expressiveness.

EXAMPLE: *Filmkunskap II*

In his teaching films, the Swedish script editor Ola Olsson shows how it is possible to create an *illusory* continuity of space, time, and action by cutting on the direction of a movement or a look.

Shots 1, 3, and 5 show Superman (Brasse Brännström) running toward the left and then climbing a tree. Shots 2 and 4 show a tiger running in the same direction. We get the impression that the tiger is chasing Superman.

The shots of the tiger were taken at Kolmården Safari Park and Superman was shot at Gärdet, a park in Stockholm.

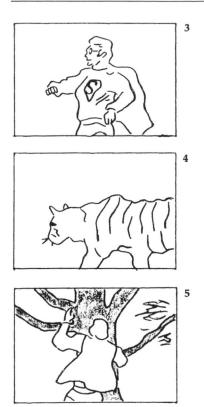

In order to create this illusory continuity, only _one_ of the settings must be established—in this case the safari park. Superman is then edited against a neutral green background that does not reveal his true whereabouts. _The lack_ of any other point of reference makes us place him in the same setting as the tiger. In this way the spectator sees a logical sequence of events that never existed in any real situation.

EXAMPLE: Chaplin's _The Circus_

In this film, Charlie Chaplin accidentally goes into a lion's cage and cannot get out. Shot 1 shows Chaplin and the lion _in the same shot._ So, too, does shot 4, where we even see a dog, which stops outside the cage and barks. In shot 2, when we see only the lion, we are more aware of the danger it represents because we have

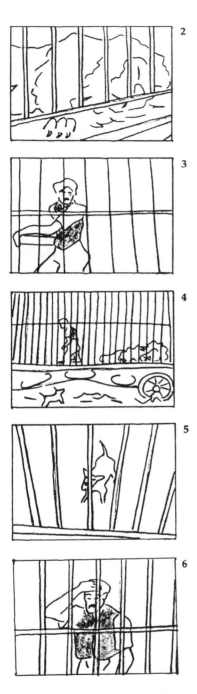

seen Chaplin and the lion in physical proximity to each other. This fact also influences shots 3, 5, and 6, even though these were certainly made without the lion present. Chaplin, then, increases the tension by *establishing* a physical proximity that is real and not brought about just by editing.

Nowadays in most scenes where an animal chases somebody, we want to see at least *one* shot in which both animal and human appear together. This is often sufficient to maintain the credibility of the remaining faked action.

EXAMPLE: Antonioni's *The Outcry*

A cutting style that differs radically from, for instance, Hitchcock's "captivating" technique can be seen in the work of Antonioni, and nowhere is this more apparent than in his *The Outcry*. The scene illustrated is a heart-to-heart talk between Aldo and the woman he has lived with for many years. We see them on the banks of the river Po. Aldo tries to find out why Irma has been behaving so strangely. Antonioni observes them from a distance—in a two-shot (shot 1). Cut to another angle on them both, where Irma says they have to reach a decision (2a). Aldo does not understand, he gets up impatiently, the camera picks him out alone for a few seconds against the grey river, then he returns to the shot of them both. When Irma says that one of them has drifted away from the other, she leans backward so that her head is hidden by the trunk of the tree. Then she stands up and the camera follows her alone (2b). She tells him that she has found someone else. At the same time, we hear the film's melancholic musical theme on the piano.

3a is another shot of them both; Irma takes a few steps to the right. Aldo grabs her arm and looks as though he wants to hit her (3b). But he calms down and walks with her up to the house where they live. We can see here how Antonioni consistently avoids using *cutting* to create drama. He keeps the camera at a distance from the characters (even at the most poignant moments, e.g., shot 3b).

Most directors would have elected to accentuate a key scene like this one by using shot and reverse shot, varying the size of the shots to emphasize the shifts in dramatic tension between the characters. Antonioni avoids taking sides in this way. Instead, he lets the composition of the shots and the physical relations between persons and objects comment on the action. The important thing is not the dramatic effect but the thematic comment. When the characters are masked by a tree trunk, when they touch each other, move away from each other, turn their backs, etc., this *expresses* something about their relationship. In other words, we have to *read* the picture (especially the composition and the bodily constellations) in order to get into the situation. This *detached* involvement incessantly appeals to our ability to reflect. The emotional effect is by no means absent; it is created by Antonioni's masterly control of mood. However, an emotional insight is created by way of our capacity to reflect. Thus it ingrains itself deeper than the effects of an evocative cutting technique.

EXAMPLE: Welles' *Citizen Kane*

In *Citizen Kane*, Orson Welles developed a *deep-focus style* whereby he was able to maintain picture definition in both foreground and background. In this way he was able to work with elements at varying depths of the picture *simultaneously* without having to cut between them. Dramatic tension could be created *within* the shot instead of by cutting *between* shots. In shot 1a we see Charles Kane as a boy, playing in the snow with a sled. The camera moves back slightly to reveal that the shot has been taken through a window. Kane's mother's head appears in the foreground and she calls out to Kane (1b). The camera then tracks back a long way and stops on the other side of the room. The mother follows the camera and sits down in the foreground on the right-hand edge of the frame. Thatcher, the banker, sits down beside her. Toward the left of the frame, in the middle ground, stands Kane's father.

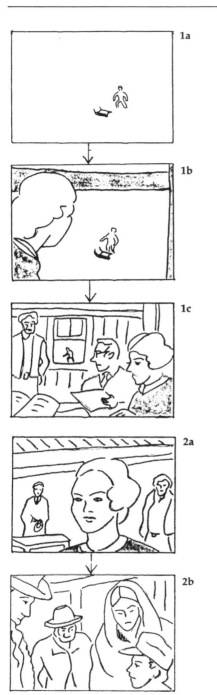

Between them, far in the background, we can still see Kane, who is playing outside the window (1c).

The relationship between the characters here is expressed by means of dynamic shifts in composition. The mother, who is the dominant person, takes up the most prominent position in the right foreground. Thatcher, who sides with her, takes his place in her part of the picture. The father, who in vain tries to protest against the decision that is about to be made, is pushed away toward the left, farther to the rear. *Between* them we see Kane, who is the subject of the discussion. He is far off in the background and has no say in the matter whatever.

When the father makes his final attempt to protest, he comes to the foreground but is immediately defeated by the argument of his wife and Thatcher. The next instant he *masks* the boy when he goes and shuts the window. The boy's own wishes are completely blotted out.

In shot 2a we see the mother (who has opened the window again) in a dominating position between the father and Thatcher. She calls out to Kane and the camera

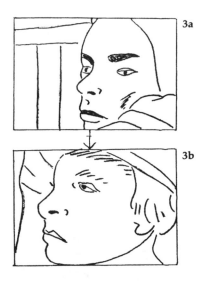

pulls back to an exterior shot as the three of them come out to talk to the boy.

In the composition of the shot, Kane is "surrounded" by his mother on the right, Thatcher on the left, and his father in the background. When Kane seeks refuge with his mother, he places himself completely in her part of the shot (2b). The scene closes with a close-up of the mother (3a), which tilts to a close-up of Kane (3b). He stares at Thatcher with hatred in his eyes. The close-up is used here to lend extra dramatic weight and round off the scene.

Here, Welles uses picture composition and physical relations in order to *comment* on the events in long, unbroken takes. This makes for dynamic tension that changes constantly. As in the Antonioni example, we follow events at a *reflective distance*. This element of observation and reflection would have been broken if the sequence had been edited in conventional "Dallas style." Emotion and intellect here have the opportunity to work in a parallel way. This would have been made much more difficult if the sequence had been edited in order to make us identify with the characters. Welles' view of reality is much more complex. Consequently, he makes more demands on the spectators.

STRUCTURAL
AND DRAMATIC
TECHNIQUES

9
THE SCENE

In film terminology, a distinction is often made between *scene* and *sequence*, but in practice they are used to mean the same thing. Here, scene means a complete, continuous chain of actions that happens in the same place and at the same time. (Some people define sequence as a group of scenes that are linked together by a definable common thread of action.)

Our perception of the scene is determined not only by the action contained in it but also by what precedes it (what *leads up to* it) and by what follows (what the scene *leads to*). The function of the scene is to carry the action forward (especially in drama) and/or to increase the audience's insight and understanding (especially in the epic form). If, after a scene, we do not feel that something has changed (relationships, objectives, attitudes—including perhaps our own attitudes as an audience, our understanding), then the scene is probably a bad choice and acts as a vacuum in the film.

When constructing the scene, three factors must be defined: *action, function, and form.*

Action

What happens in the scene? *Who* does what and *why?* What *preconditions* exist for what happens in the scene? Are they already established by preceding scenes or must they be given during the course of the scene itself? In most cases where new information must be introduced, it should be given as *early* as possible or the action can easily become unclear or incomprehensible. The exception is when certain conditions come as a surprise at the end of the scene (the charming gentleman who turns out to be a Blue-beard). The preconditions should give the scene a uniform *direction*—they must lead the action to an end or to a turning point that creates new preconditions for the successive scenes. It is important to choose a *point of attack* (often *in medias res*—well into the action), which, without unnecessary delay, sets the course of the scene. In drama, the driving power behind this course is nearly always the *sub-text*, i.e., the real motives and objectives that make people behave as they do, without being openly admitted or expressed in the dialogue. The sub-text should be indirectly discernible only from what the characters do and their reactions to other people—it should never be placed in the characters' mouths in the form of explanatory lines. (See "Dialogue"). Tensions and disturbances often lead to a release, which, in turn, gives rise to new tensions and new disturbances. Consequently, the scene is often a kind of *mini-drama* within the drama (in the epic form, the scene is a sort of subordinate analysis within the whole field of the problem) with an exposition of the problem, development of conflict, climax, and resolution.

Function

The function of the scene is determined by its position in the dramatic or epic whole. In drama, each scene should lead the conflict toward its final solution. In the epic form, the scene should clarify the problem that is being examined, throw new light on it, and increase our insight into it. In addition to this, the function of the scene is to support the *central idea* (see below) of the film or program in both drama and epic.

Form

Once the action and the function of the scene have been established, the most important task remains: to find a means of expression that will make the scene stand out in the most effective way and fix it organically to the film as a whole. In other words, the *elements of narrative* must be exploited in a consistent and deliberate way. Within the bounds of the style we are working with, emotion and information must be manipulated with the *end result* we wish to achieve in mind. This means, first of all, that we should *say enough without saying too much*. If we say or show too little, the audience will miss the point; if we say or show too much, the audience will anticipate the point. In either case the effect is lost. Basically, this is a matter of finding the formal _twist_ that presents the material in an unexpected yet perfectly acceptable way. Finding the twist is (or ought to be) the most difficult part of the creative process. It would be futile to try to lay down rules for doing this; we shall never get anywhere without imagination and free creative talent. The real art lies in finding new twists. Imitation is soon exposed as mere mimicry and affectation.

10
CHARACTER

In feature films and TV plays, we express what we want to say, i.e., the *dramatic truth* we want to demonstrate, largely through the characters. Therefore, choosing characters who can carry out this task without seeming to act against themselves and their conditions is of the utmost importance. The audience should not have the impression that the author is somewhere behind the scenes pulling the strings; the characters' actions must be logical and consistent with their attributes and conditions. The attributes of the characters who influence the drama must be drawn accurately. Even complex characters must appear *complete*. (One common fault is to draw characters in a vague way to avoid stereotypes; the result is blurred characters with neither profile nor individuality. Ambiguous and complex characters are not created by fuzziness but by a combination of contradictory traits that are each clearly drawn.) There is no need to say *everything* about a person for the audience to appreciate the many sides of the *whole* person. We must try to present the important traits in such a way that the audience spontaneously associates a whole series of other traits which will make the character seem complete and real. Schematically, the fictional character can be represented in this way:

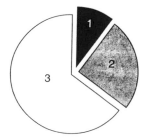

1. What we actually *learn* about the person
2. What we can *deduce* about the person
3. Everything we *do not need to know* about the person.

Example: In one scene a businessman speaks contemptuously about the Peace Movement and declares that he would rather be dead than Red. Conclusions about his other political views—perhaps even his attitude toward raising children, school reports, and so on—can be fairly safely drawn. But in this context, whether he prefers Mozart to Beethoven or spaghetti to hamburgers is completely irrelevant. We can _complicate_ the character by allowing unexpected traits to contradict the stereotyped image. (For example, he may be an extreme left-winger, like certain factions of the Marxist-Leninist movement in Norway who are very pro-NATO and, these days, very oriented towards business.)

CHARACTER CHECKLIST

Although we only _show_ a limited range of aspects of the character, we must know everything about him. We must be able to bring out any attributes or information necessary at any time with complete confidence that the new information fits in with the character as a whole. (If we do not do this, we are not creating subtlety but confusion.) Every character must be formed _three-dimensionally_, i.e., as a product of physical, psychological and sociological attributes. (Even if all these are not overtly expressed in the film, we must be aware of them if we are to avoid flatness in characterization.) As writers, we may put together a checklist for every character. Naturally, this can be altered during the course of the work.

1) Physical data

- Sex
- Age
- Build (thin, tall, athletic) and bearing
- Attractive or unattractive physical attributes
- Color and style of hair
- Typical clothing and condition of clothing
- Gestures and mimicry
- Way of talking (accent, slang, articulation)
- Any defects (deformities, illness)

Always try to find some _easily recognizable trait_ for the person and decide what other people's _first impression_ of this person is.

2) Sociological data

- Ethnic background and nationality
- Social class
- Education
- Profession (income, working conditions)
- Living conditions
- Family (married/single, children, relations with other family members)
- Friends (at work and outside of work)
- Hobbies, interests
- Political views and affiliations
- Religious views and affiliations
- Name

3) Psychological data

- Ambitions (long and short-term objectives)
- Frustrations (everything that prevents him or her from achieving his/her objectives)
- Dreams (which the character may think unattainable)
- Personal weaknesses
- Temperament
- Intelligence
- Attitude toward life (optimistic/pessimistic, rebellious, happy, altruistic, selfish)
- Fundamental values (*concrete* expressions of what the person holds dear, e.g., family life, hard work)
- Romantic/sexual disposition
- Complexes (inhibitions, phobias, fixed ideas)
- Special talents (music, sport)

While working on the script, it is advisable to try to define the person's *dominant character trait*. While this does not give a complete description, it is often the key to the person's behavior in different circumstances and creates unity and consistency in characterization. When we have identified the dominant character trait, we can begin to create variations by introducing *secondary character traits*.

On the basis of dominant and secondary character traits, we can formulate the person's *dominant intention* both in the film as a whole and in each individual scene. Desire is the person's driving force.

A good test of whether or not we _know_ our characters is to think of them in situations where their personal attributes and characteristics would be prominent:

- at work
- with friends
- with their families
- alone

CLOSED AND OPEN CHARACTERS

In classical drama, characters are shaped so that they appear as consistent expressions of their _role functions_. They could not behave in any other way. From the attributes already established they fulfill their function within the dramatic framework with a sense of necessity. We may call these _closed_ characters. On the basis of our knowledge of their personal attributes, we can, to some extent, _foresee_, long in advance, how they will react and behave in different situations.

In modern drama, however, we often use _open characters_. They are contradictory, often illogical and enigmatic. They themselves do not know why they behave as they do. Their behavior is unpredictable. Consequently, they are less suited to tight dramatic plots. Open characters are more at home in certain _epic_ portrayals where people themselves are _unknown_ quantities that are subjected to analysis (see, for instance, Bergman's _From the Life of the Marionettes_).

We could enlarge upon the distinction by saying that, whereas the author of a conventional _drama_ needs to know _everything_ about his characters, the very point of certain _epic_ portrayals is the fact that the author does _not_ know this (see, for instance, some of Antonioni's and Resnais' films). He approaches his characters from the outside, observes them, interprets them. The director Peter Brook has said about his film _Moderato Cantabile_ (based on a novel by Marguerite Duras): "The basic mystery will remain hidden and impenetrable for the spectator, just as it is for Marguerite Duras and for myself."

Just _what_ moves open (epic) characters to act as they do must be inferred by the spectator on the basis of his own experience and understanding of the kind of world that is represented in the film.

PRESENTATION OF CHARACTER TRAITS

In films and TV plays people are never anything other than *what they do*. A trait of character exists only insofar as it is seen *in action*. A concrete, specific, *visual* means of expression must be found even for the most complex and hidden attributes. Nothing is more devastating (from the point of view of drama) than nonspecific, free-floating *states of mind* where an actor is required to show an emotion or a change of emotion without having anything to react to that causes the emotion.

Character traits can, for example, be shown in the following ways:

1) through action (*what* the person tries to do and *how* he tries to do it)
2) through reaction (how the person reacts to new situations and to what other people do)
3) through the reactions of *others*
4) through dialogue (particularly what the person does *not* say, what he hides; incidentally, his *way* of speaking is just as important as *what* he says)
5) through his appearance, clothes, and characteristic patterns of behavior
6) through his relationship to props
7) through his relationship to his setting
8) through contrast with what others do
9) through name

A trait of character is often enhanced if the person is allowed to display minor traits which *contradict* the main attribute. (A ruthless man is more dangerous if he is shown to be thoughtful and loving in certain situations.)

11

DIALOGUE

Many a good film story is weakened by poor dialogue. It is one of the aspects of film-narrative that is most difficult to master.

The most common error is to load the dialogue with *too much information*. Too much has to be explained; the situations do not work without long-winded explanations of conditions, thoughts, and intentions. This means that the dramatic situation has not been clearly molded.

One good way of getting it right is *first* to try to write the scene with no dialogue at all. This helps to give a clear idea of the essential dramatic framework of the scene. What is the purpose of the scene? What do the characters *want*? What actually *happens*? Can this be shown through physical action, gesture, looks, props, setting? If these elements can be made to work so that the drama and the thematic content take form, it will be noticed that the dialogue flows more easily and naturally. Much of what was originally put in the mouths of the characters can be dispensed with. Those words that remain should spring unbidden from the situations without the need to *explain* them.

THE FUNCTIONS OF DIALOGUE

1. Dialogue must be *realistic and credible* in its context. When characters speak, we should have the impression that these people speak *in this way* and no other. The dialogue should grow as an organic part of the whole that is constituted by person and situation; it should not determine this whole but be *determined* by it.

2. The dialogue should *characterize the person who speaks*. The *way* he expresses himself tells us a great deal about him. Here, it is not the literal meaning of what he says that matters. Equally important is the emotional significance of the words, what they conceal, and so on.

3. The dialogue must express the speaker's *mood*. Here, too, the *way* it is expressed is more important than the words spoken.

4. The dialogue should characterize the person being spoken *to* or *about*. If we see a person who is disdainful and insolent toward everybody but becomes cautious and respectful when a certain person appears, the newcomer does not need to say or do anything. He has already taken form as someone very special. Similarly, we can learn a lot about people from what is said in their absence.

5. The dialogue should *move the action forward*, i.e., it should be a driving force in the drama. It should, in the words of the Swedish actor, author, and director Henrik Dyfverman, "touch someone, affect someone, provoke someone, have some effect on events, either in particular or in general."

6. Dialogue should *give information*. But the information should come naturally from the context and not be placed in the mouths of the characters. Nothing is worse than giving the audience the impression that the characters are speaking the author's words.

WRITING DIALOGUE

First of all, dialogue should sound *natural* and not made up. But good film dialogue is not a mechanical rendering of natural speech. Everyday speech is full of repetition and superfluity—it contains too many words and inessentials. Film dialogue requires *selection, concentration, and compactness*. Film dialogue *simulates* real speech but does not *copy* it.

It must also be based on *oral* rather than written forms. Film dialogue is not grammatically correct. It is not an academic treatise but the expression of vital, thinking, feeling people of flesh and blood.

Every line should be *characteristic* of the speaker. When we read his lines in the script, we should have the impression that nobody else would speak in quite the same way.

As a general rule, the *emotional* content of the line is more important than the literal meanings of the words.

Good dialogue is often *disconnected and illogical.* We do not behave in a logical way. We do not speak in syllogisms. What we say is part of a contradictory whole that is our personality, in a world full of uncertainties. As Dyfverman says: "Living madness is better than dead logic."

Gestures, exclamations, and actions should take the place of the spoken word wherever possible.

The *intensity* of the dialogue should reflect the intensity of the situation. A less intense scene permits dialogue that is more discursive. In a dramatically heightened situation, the dialogue is more compressed and spare.

The characters in a play or film do not speak in order to give information (if they do there is reason to believe they are lying); they speak in order to influence the attitudes and behavior of others. Dramatic speech presupposes and creates conflict. Dyfverman says, "A play is about a crisis, a scene is about a crisis in the crisis, and the lines about a series of crises within this crisis." The give and take of lines is a matter of action and reaction, counter-action and counter-reaction. Dyfverman explains: "Good dialogue reaps and sows at the same time. The solution to one problem causes another, a knot when undone leaves a loop that, perhaps only much later, tightens to become a new knot."

People must not give information voluntarily and *never* without reason. Let the information be obtained by provocation, threats, force, cajoling and always against a certain amount of resistance, for the purpose of drama is to *force* the truth out. If there is no resistance, there is no drama. As writer Dwight Swain says, "Fiction is friction."

Never let a character give information about something his interlocutor must know already. Try rather to insert into the drama conditions that will reveal the information in a natural way.

Dramatic dialogue is *never conversation.* The speakers must never talk as if they were discussing the latest news. Abstract and general debate kills dialogue instantly. Good film dialogue is about matters that have a direct effect on the speakers.

Lines should be written so that they say *one thing at a time.* The following line is a textbook example of how a line should *not* be written: "Yes, but surely one should consider people's anxiety and fear as well." That is TV debate, not dialogue. The sentence contains a statement and a question: a statement about how people feel and a question regarding what should be done about it. So it should be split into two shorter lines where question and statement are separated, e.g., "People are scared. Should we ignore that?"

The lines should be as *short* as possible, and any superfluous words should be dropped. In the example above, it is unnecessary to use both "anxiety" and "fear"; simply choose the strongest of the two.

A sentence does not need to be complete. It can be cut short by the interlocutor or ended of its own accord because of a sudden feeling that enough has already been said.

Connecting words ("and," "because," "although," etc.) should be avoided. Short sentences work best; clauses only complicate things.

Words that reinforce have no place in dialogue. "I'm scared" is better than "I'm very scared." The reinforcement should be in the situation, not in the dialogue.

TEXT AND SUB-TEXT

By "text" we mean the *wording* of the dialogue, the conventional meaning of the words. *Sub-text* refers to the *deeper veiled meaning* behind the words. The sub-text is in the real—and often unspoken—rapport between the characters, in the hidden meaning of what they say and do. It refers to the true intentions and goals of the characters.

We *are* always much more than we say. When we speak, we do not reveal everything about ourselves. In relation to what we are, feel, desire, and want, we express only a small part or nothing at all. Words act as a mask or cover over our true intentions. They hide as much as—or more than—they express.

Drama exists in order to bring out the *truth* about people. The dramatic process should bring it *to the surface.* There is resistance to this. Good dramatic dialogue does not speak the sub-text except at the moment when the truth comes out, which usually happens near the climax. A good rule of drama is that *people always lie.* There is tension between what they say and what they really feel, mean, and want. All the same, the sub-text is there in the words but it is indirect, disguised. The highest level of dramatic tension is achieved when the text (a) *alludes to* or (b) *contradicts* the sub-text.

In order for the text to work well, the audience must *understand the sub-text.* They must be aware of the meaning behind the words or the dramatic tension is lost. It is always a challenge for an actor to *play against the sub-text* (both in word and deed) in such a way that the sub-text (seemingly against his will) is revealed.

In drama, it is the sub-text and not the text that should hang together. The dialogue itself does not need to be, indeed should not be, logical and connected, but the underlying situation must be so. Dialogue can take off in all directions and be about any subject under the sun as long as the sub-text is clear and strong (i.e., moves the drama forward).

Example: In Tony Garnett's pseudo-documentary *Prostitute*, a sociologist invites a colleague home. The colleague is a woman social worker. We have already seen that they are attracted to each other. Now they are sitting drinking wine. The sociologist is inhibited and shy and is talking in dry and scholarly terms about prostitution. The closer they come to the moment of truth (it's getting late), the more abstract his intellectual observations become. In the end, the woman lays her hand on his knee and says, "Let's go to bed." The ice is broken; she has expressed the sub-text. (Notice that the text *alludes* to the sub-text throughout. He talks about physical love but not between *them*.)

The same intention (sub-text) can be expressed in many different ways (text). Schematically represented, it could look like this:

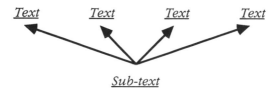

The sub-text *I love you* can be expressed with the words "I love you" or "I hate you." In the latter case, the words *contradict* the sub-text (e.g., in a lover's moment of disappointment).

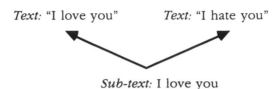

Text: "I love you"   Text: "I hate you"

Sub-text: I love you

The *same* text can also have different meanings (sub-text). The text "I love you" can mean both *I love you* and *I hate you*.

Text: "I love you"

Sub-text: I love you   Sub-text: I hate you

It is the dramatic situation (i.e., the true relation between the characters) that determines the actual meaning of the words.

Taking an analogy from psychology and psychiatry, we can say that the text represents the *visible symptom* while the sub-text is the underlying concealed *cause of the illness.* The *same cause* can find expression in many different symptoms. A good writer chooses symptoms that hint at the cause (sub-text) *without directly expressing it.*

(In psychoanalysis we talk about *manifest expression* (visible) and *latent meaning* (not visible). This exactly expresses the relationship between what we call text and sub-text.)

Often in classical drama, the nearer we come to the climax, the nearer the sub-text comes to the surface (i.e., becomes text). Lies are no longer possible; the painful truth must be faced. The characters, at last, speak "from their hearts" (i.e., sub-text). All the implications of the conflict are now expressed openly. (Nora in *A Doll's House*: "It's time to throw off the costumes.") Will stands openly against will. Both parties have put their cards on the table. All that remains now is the test of strength.

12
SPINE CONSTRUCTION

THE SUBJECT

The first thing to decide before starting work on a film or TV program is its subject. What is the film or program about? The more comprehensive, complex, and difficult the problem is, the harder it is to define its limits. It tends to grow as we dig more deeply into it. There is often the temptation, for the sake of objectivity, to get everything in that is remotely relevant to the topic. This often leads to the material getting out of hand; it cannot be organized into a comprehensible and coherent whole. If we try to juggle too many balls, we lose them all. If we try to say *everything*, we end up saying nothing at all. We simply sit there with a muddle of information.

As a guiding principle, then, for making thematic choices, the *main subject* must be formulated from the very start. It is important to formulate it as precisely as possible *in words*; this makes it easier to define limits and saves a lot of unnecessary work. For example, is the program to be about play? As a definition of the subject, this is far too broad. Children's play? That's better. What is it that particularly interests us in children's play enough to make us want to make a program about it? Creativity? Individuality? Imagination? Now we are getting down to something we can get a hold of. Perhaps we want to say something about conformity, or we might just be interested in how individual creativity can be encouraged through play. Both could be our main subject. (We must be careful, however, to choose only one of them.) But what if we are interested in the *conflict* between these two aspects? Then we can formulate our main subject as follows: "Conformity versus creativity as expressed through children's play."

It is important that the program has a single main subject. This main subject guarantees the unity of the program. Anything that does not exemplify, submit to or throw light on the main subject must be removed ruthlessly. It can, however, be a good idea to illustrate the main subject with *secondary themes* that throw relevant light on the main subject. For example, we can define the problem of creativity and conformity in children's play by considering adult sport. This kind of digression may enable us to return to the main problem with more pertinent questions. But the secondary theme must not be allowed to develop into *another main subject* or the program will be pulling in different directions and unity will be lost. If you try to ride two horses at the same time, you fall off both.

The subject simply tells us *what* the film or program will be about; it says nothing about *what we want to say*, nothing about the insights or attitudes we wish to promote. This is the task of the *central idea*.

THE CENTRAL IDEA

While the main subject and the secondary themes define the matters of reality we are working with, they say nothing about the *stance we take* toward these matters. But the very reason why we want to make a program about something is—or at least should be—that we are involved, that we have opinions about it, that we want to present certain insights into it that are important to us. We have an *attitude* toward the subject of the program that is based on certain *values*. These values are the basis of the *choices* we make while working on the program. It is impossible to treat a subject without making value-choices; values lie behind every choice of camera angle, every cut, every sequence of shots, and so on. The attempt to hide this is often called "objectivity," but this word is a mystification in audio-visual contexts. The only thing we can and should strive for is *pertinence*, and we do this best if we are aware of our values and *render an account of them*. It is then up to us to argue our position in a way that openly presents the problem and hides nothing from the audience.

We may formulate the stance adopted by the filmmaker toward the subject of the film in terms of a *central idea*. Like the main subject, the central idea must be formulated in words; it can be said to be the shortest possible formulation of what the filmmaker is trying to say. The central idea expresses the essential *insight* that the filmmaker wishes to impart to the spectator. It is not and can never be an incontrovertible scientific truth; it is always based on overt or covert values.

The central idea lends the key to the structure of the program. It determines what we are going to emphasize and what is to be ignored; it determines the order of the various parts, how we use the various narrative elements, how we begin, develop, and end the program.

In a program about children's play, our point of view might be that children develop toward conformity if they do not have opportunities for play that take into consideration their own needs, creativity and imagination. This will do as a central idea. But it is not an incontrovertible truth. It is an insight, an opinion that we, as program makers, must present in such a way that the audience will find it *reasonable*. We must try to be convincing by means of well-chosen examples and plausible argument.

A program without a strong central idea is trivial—it has no direction, no core, no conviction. It is indifferent and uninteresting.

THE CENTRAL IDEA IN DRAMA

In dramatic productions (feature films, TV plays, docudramas) the central idea is often called the *premise*. The drama promotes the central idea or premise through *action* that substantially (on the Plane of Events) "proves" the premise. The premise always has two constituent parts: it formulates (a) preconditions and (b) consequences. It says, *Condition X leads to consequence Y.* In other words, the premise is *dynamic*. It sets action in motion. The premise is inherent in the development of the action.

Example: The subject of Ibsen's *A Doll's House* can be said to be "moral inequality in marriage." There can be various opinions on this theme. For example, one might think that men are morally superior to women and that a wife should therefore submit to her husband's moral judgement. Many people believed so when the play was written (some still might even today). Ibsen, however, was not of this opinion. His position vis à vis the subject was expressed in the play and can be formulated thus: "Moral inequality in marriage leads to the destruction of marriage." Moral inequality is the precondition that, through the dramatic situations in the play, has, as a consequence, the destruction of marriage.

In the formulation of the premise

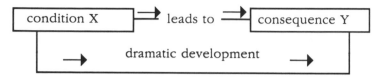

both X and Y should be specified in concrete terms. The premise is never abstract and general ("life is a dream" is no dramatic premise) but always concrete and specific ("ruthless ambition leads to ruin"—a tight and simple premise for Shakespeare's *Macbeth*).

THE CENTRAL IDEA IN EPIC STRUCTURES

While drama demonstrates the viability of the central idea through the actual development of the action, in investigative and problem-posing films (treated here under the heading of *epic* structure—see later chapters) the central idea often takes the form of a *question*. A documentary filmmaker who wants to discover why the suicide rate among children in Sweden is so high does not know the answer already. The filmmaker *only knows section Y* of the dramatic premise (consequence Y = the high suicide rate among children). What are the conditions, i.e., section X? He does not know yet, and that is the question he is trying to answer in the film. The guiding question is then: "What is the reason for the high rate of suicide among children in Sweden?" He can only set out a *hypothesis* about it, and this hypothesis is a tentative answer to the question he asks. It may be necessary to modify the hypothesis several times during the course of the work. It may, for example, be, "Is the high rate of suicide among children caused by alcohol?" During the course of his work he may find a connection but not an answer. He has to pose a *new hypothesis* about the reasons behind both the suicides and the consumption of alcohol (bad living conditions? and so on) until it is reasonable to conclude the inquiry. He can never expect to find a definite answer but he might find a *pattern*, a series of different interconnections that together form a whole. It is his task as a filmmaker to *interpret* this whole. When editing the material, he may be able to formulate a premise that encompasses all the various contexts (e.g., "lack of social interaction leads to child suicide") but, there again, he may not. It may be better to construct the program as *a gradual examination of the guiding* _question_ ("What is the reason for the high suicide rate among children?"), where each step illustrates and leads us further toward the core of the problem, but where the core itself is never reached—maybe because it is not there. Perhaps the answer we are looking for cannot be formulated in a simple statement. The _insight_ we have reached, thanks to various partial answers and partial illustrations, might be that the problem is more complicated than we first thought. We have given the audience the relevant data and reference points for them to formulate their own answers.

Unity in a dramatic structure is created by the _premise_ of the dramatic action (that is to say, on the Plane of Events), while unity in an epic structure is created by the logic of the epic inquiry itself (i.e., on the Plane of Discourse). The premise in a drama is always a _statement_ about a state of affairs; the guiding question in an epic inquiry is often a _putting in question_ of this same sort of statement.

Example: Our point of departure is a dramatic premise: "Crime leads to punishment." Many dramatic productions have shown this, especially in films. We now make a problem of the statement and start out with a question: "Does crime always lead to punishment or does it depend on the sort of crime and who the criminals are?" As a next step, we set out a hypothesis that we test against reality, e.g., "Is it true that monetary crimes are punished lightly or not at all?" The result of the inquiry will determine whether we need to delve further, put up new hypotheses, examine other types of crime, and so on. As a result of the examination, we might possibly wish to propose a more provocative central idea than the tentative question we started out with and organize the program around this, e.g., "If you have enough money and good lawyers, you can make crime pay." Or else we can organize the material in accordance with the guiding question, present the relevant data and findings to the audience in a logical and orderly whole, and let them draw their own conclusions.

To sum up:

In a _dramatic structure_, the central idea takes the form of a _premise_ (X leads to Y) that is given shape through the development of the dramatic situations on the Plane of Events.

In an _epic structure_, the central idea often (but not always) takes the form of a _guiding question_ that we attempt to answer by proposing relevant _hypotheses_ that are tested against reality (whether the reality be fictional or factual). As a consequence of the inquiry, we can either formulate a more viable central idea or retain the guiding question as the structural principle of the film.

PREMISE CONSTRUCTION: INGOLF GABOLD'S MODEL

As discussed on the preceding pages, the central idea of a film or TV program can take the form of a dramatic premise that, like a dynamic motor, determines the development of the action in the film. Schematically, we expressed it like this:

> X leads to Y

X represents the *dramatic preconditions* that instigate a series of events whose *consequence* is Y. E.g., poverty (X) leads to crime (Y).

Formulated in this way, the premise is very vague and general. It only gives the starting point and the finishing point for the person or persons in the film who, through their own development, will "prove" the validity of the premise. We show, for example, how an honest citizen, Mr. A, loses his job and his money and turns to crime as a means of survival. His story expresses and supports the premise.

But we know full well that not all poor people become criminals. In this bald form, the formulation of the premise says nothing about the *circumstances* under which poverty leads to crime. The formula "X leads to Y" gives the *direction* but says nothing about why "Y" is reached in some cases but not in others.

Danish writer Ingolf Gabold has tried to find a remedy for this lack of precision. As we shall see, Gabold's model has the advantage of *specifying precisely those conditions that determine the dramatic development and resolution* in every concrete film. Because of this, the model can help the writer/filmmaker to concentrate on essentials and ensure that the film really says what it is intended to say.

If we take Gillo Pontecorvo's *The Battle of Algiers* as an example, we can define the overall premise of development as follows:

Oppression (X) leads to revolt (Y)

This indicates the consistent direction of the film, from the starting point (political ignorance and apathy) to the final state of things (self-determination as a consequence of mass revolt). The premise tells us *where we are going* but says nothing about the conditions necessary to achieve the aim. In the film the organized resistance is crushed, but a collective uprising toward the end of the film results in victory. The film shows that oppression causes revolt, although certain conditions must be fulfilled if the revolt is to be successful.

With Gabold's model, it is easier to identify the conditions that are dramatically decisive. The skeleton of his premise construction looks like this:

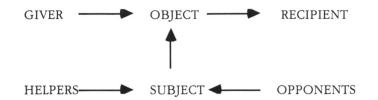

The vertical axis represents the DRAMATIC SUBJECT and the DRA-MATIC AIM (OBJECT). Gabold calls it the "subject/object axis." (We could also call it the *dynamic axis*: it shows the direction of the film.) The dramatic subject is the role-function we shall discuss elsewhere as the protagonist or principal role, that is to say the role-figure that embodies the premise on its way to the dramatic aim. It is important to decide *who* the dramatic subject (protagonist) is from the very beginning as it is through this role that we determine the dramatic aim, thus indicating the central thrust of the film. The dramatic subject in *The Battle of Algiers* it is not altogether clear, at first glance. Consequently, our understanding of the premise of the film will vary according to who we perceive as the dramatic subject.

Let us first choose Ali-la-Pointe as the subject and see what happens. It seems a reasonable choice—Ali is the person who undergoes the greatest visible development in the film, from political apathy to self-sacrificing solidarity. We can fix Ali's dramatic aim as "freedom for Algeria." The "subject/object axis" then looks like this:

Gabold says the subject/object axis is an axis of DESIRE that shows what our subject is striving for—what our subject wants.

From the subject/object axis, we can trace a horizontal CONFLICT axis, showing which dynamic forces are working in *favor* of the subject's desires and which are working *against* them. The forces working in favor are set out on the left of the axis under the heading HELPERS. These can be people, forces of nature, social conditions, laws, ideologies, and so on. On the right, under the heading OPPONENTS, we set out all the forces that work *against* the subject. What we then have is the *conflict area* in which the subject will have to move.

Without doubt, Ali's most important helper in *The Battle of Algiers* is the FLN (the Resistance). He also has support in the Casbah (with its labyrinthine geography), from certain journalists, from certain quarters in the U.N., etc. His opponents are, above all, the French colonial power (with its representatives: civil, military, and political). We can present the axis of conflict like this:

HELPERS ➤	SUBJECT ◀	OPPONENTS
Terrorist methods of the FLN, civilian sympathizers, liberal journalists, certain people in the U.N., etc.	Ali-la-Pointe	The French population of Algeria, police and military forces, "political will" in France, etc.

All dramatic constructions have *something specific* that, in the end, determines whether the subject is going to achieve the dramatic aim. *What* the writer/filmmaker chooses to emphasize is of the utmost importance to our understanding the "message" or the "moral" of the film. Consequently, starting from the subject/object axis, Gabold sets out a third (horizontal) axis, where he tries to decide *what* it is that determines whether or not the dramatic aim is achieved. He calls this a "giver/recipient axis" or, more simply, an axis of COMMUNICATION. This axis shows *who or what* makes it possible for the RECIPIENT to achieve the objective (the dramatic aim).

In *The Battle of Algiers*, we have defined the objective as "freedom for Algeria." In the film, the dramatic subject, Ali, does not see the achievement of this aim. Only in the final scenes do the

Algerian people attain the objective (freedom for Algeria) as a result of a collective mass revolt. The "axis of communication" might then look like this:

Collective national revolt — GIVER → Freedom for Algeria — OBJECT → The Algerian people — RECIPIENT

We may "read" this axis as follows: "Only by a collective, national revolt can the Algerian people achieve their freedom."

We can now set out the complete model:

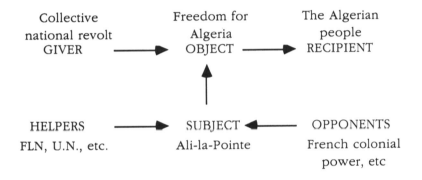

Collective national revolt — GIVER → Freedom for Algeria — OBJECT → The Algerian people — RECIPIENT

HELPERS FLN, U.N., etc. → SUBJECT Ali-la-Pointe ← OPPONENTS French colonial power, etc

On the basis of this arrangement, the premise can be put into words as follows:

"Despite opposition from a superior colonial power, a freedom-fighter's self-sacrificing struggle for freedom, allied to an uncompromising resistance movement, can prepare the grounds for a collective national revolt that will bring about national independence."

This gives us a much better idea of the film and its "message" than does the general formula "oppression leads to revolt." Since we arrive at this premise on the basis of a _completed film_, our formula is, of necessity, an _interpretation_. It is reasonable but not incontrovertible to identify the "giver" as "collective national revolt," since this is what finally leads to national freedom. But we _can_ also, with corroboration in the film, identify the "giver" as "the selfless sacrifice on the part of the resistance movement" because it is the willingness of the resistance fighters to die for their country that inspires the Arab population to revolt. In this case, we are placing more emphasis on the significance of the political vanguard than on the national revolt itself. The important thing is that, in deciding who the "giver" is, we are actually deciding what the *dramatically determining factor* is in the matter of how and why the subject achieves, or fails to achieve, the dramatic aim. Instead of "giver," then, we could rather use the term DETERMINANT. *It is by deciding on the "dramatic determinant" that we decide which factors are of conclusive significance in resolving the dramatic conflicts.*

In the above example, we have identified a "positive" determinant; it belongs, therefore, on the "helpers'" side of the conflict axis. It "gives" the dramatic objective (freedom) to the intended recipient (the Algerian people).

But we could also imagine a *negative* determinant. In this case, the conflicts end *tragically*—the subject fails to attain the dramatic aim.

Suppose that *The Battle of Algiers* had ended with the death of Ali-la-Pointe (as the last of the resistance leaders) at the hands of the French soldiers. The film would then have been like a classic Greek Tragedy and the premise would have looked something like this:

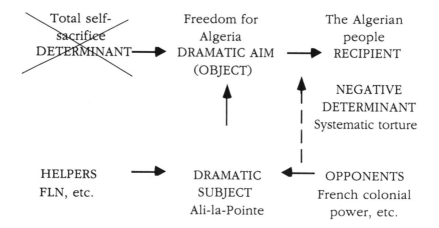

The action of the dramatic subject (total self-sacrifice, giving up his life for his country) proves *insufficient* to reach the dramatic aim (freedom). Consequently, we can cross it out. The special methods of the opponents (in this case the French soldiers' methods of torture) are so strong and effective that they *prevent* the subject from attaining the dramatic aim (freedom). In other words, the methods of torture are the *determinant* of the victory of the opponents. We can show this in the model by drawing a dotted

line from the opponents' axis to the recipient axis to indicate that
the opponent _takes_ the object _from_ the intended recipient. The
dotted line shows _what_ it is that eventually enables the opponent
to succeed, and so we call this the NEGATIVE DETERMINANT—
in this case the torture. On the basis of the model, we can formulate the following premise for this "tragic" variation of the film:

"Despite organized resistance and the readiness to sacrifice everything, it is not possible for a freedom-fighter to lead his people to national independence if his opponents meet violence with
methods that are even more ruthless and brutal."

This premise would suit a film that is anti-violence or anti-war.

As we said earlier, Ali-la-Pointe is not necessarily the dramatic
subject of the film. It could just as easily be the _Algerian people._
In this case, Ali moves to the Helper side. The model would then
look like this:

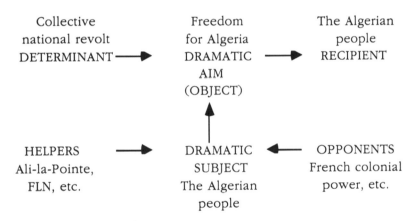

which can give the following premise:

"Despite opposition from a superior colonial power, it is possible for an oppressed people, inspired by the example of an organized resistance movement, to rally to a collective revolt that will
bring about national independence."

We see here that the emphasis is on the collective effort rather
than the individual. The fact that this premise fits the film as well
as the premise we constructed first probably means that the film
is inconsistent in its choice of dramatic subject; Ali-la-Pointe is completely missing from the film for lengthy periods, and at other times
his development is central. This creates a lack of evenness and
stringency in the construction and, for example, makes the last

fifteen minutes, where we see the uprising, seem like a separate film within the film. We could have one premise for the first 105 minutes of the film and another for the last fifteen, and this, as we know too well, means that we are on unsafe ground; a film should have only *one premise.*

THE STRUCTURAL IDEA

By way of subject and central idea we define and determine the content of a film or program. With the help of a *structural idea* we create a *form* for the program that strengthens and clarifies the subject matter and the central idea as much as possible. We might also call it the "aesthetic key," the principle of form through which the content is given concrete shape, or rather the formal *screen* through which we *see* it.

Even the most exciting and compelling subject matter can be killed by aesthetic laxity, ignorance, or lack of imagination. Films and TV programs that we remember have all had that extra something that makes them fresh and exciting, even when we see them several times over. It is not a question of a superficial aesthetic varnish but a principle of form that unites content and form indivisibly. The editing in Resnais' *Hiroshima Mon Amour* unites past and present in such a way that the theme of the film—the power of the past over the present and the inevitability of oblivion—is clearly expressed. It is simply impossible to consider the content divorced from the form. Peter Watkins' film on Munch is more than just the biography of a painter, thanks to the narrative devices Watkins uses: interviews with the actors playing the parts (as if a TV team has dropped in on the people in their real lives), sociological comments, non-chronological editing, etc.

In the example we mentioned before about children's play, we can imagine working solely with filmed interviews with parents, nursery teachers, and psychologists intermixed with pictures of children playing. It would—unfortunately—be a typical TV program. It has virtually no form-giving element. Argument and pictures glide along and everybody says his piece. We bring it to a close with some sort of warning or maxim and nobody will ever remember seeing or hearing it.

But suppose we were to try to find a stronger structural idea. Suppose we were to give the subject matter a little *twist* so that people would sit up and take notice. In the first place, perhaps we should not present the program in the form of an illustrated report. A good idea, perhaps, might be first to observe carefully how children play and then get grown-up actors to act *as if* they were children. Perhaps then we would see what has become humdrum *through other eyes.* And not only that, people would remember the film and understand it. The basic structural idea in Hellander's *Det stora barnkalaset* (*The Great Children's Party*) was like this, and it aroused considerable enthusiasm and controversy. Most people laughed, recognized themselves, and *understood.*

13
DRAMATIC STRUCTURE

REALITY AND "DRAMATIC SPACE"

Before making a film or TV program, we have to decide whether or not to dramatize the material. This choice depends on the type and purpose of the film. In certain cases, we avoid a uniform dramatic *structure* (in favor of an epic structure) while, at the same time, being able to justify the use of certain dramatic *elements*. On the other hand, it is feasible, within the limits of a dramatic structure, to work with predominantly epic elements. Many combinations are possible; the important thing is that we know what we are doing and why we are doing it.

Dramatization means adapting reality according to certain *rules*. By and large these rules have their origin in the classical theatre. When we dramatize we make a deliberate *departure* from reality in order to put it in better *focus*. We probe, as it were, under the surface of reality to get at a truth that does not always appear at first sight. This is not a scientific but a *dramatic, artistic truth*.

Let us take an example from real life to see what distinguishes it from drama. One perfectly normal day, I am walking through the streets of Stockholm. At a junction I see a road accident—two people have to be taken to hospital. A while later I see a bitter quarrel between husband and wife. Later again, in a café, I meet a friend I have not seen for ten years who has now moved to the city. On the way home, I am almost knocked down by a moped.

In my eyes these events do not have any demonstrable connection *with each other*. The accident has nothing to do with my meeting my friend, or with the quarrel, or with the moped. The cause of one event has nothing to do with the cause of another. They are pure coincidence. If I were to try to find a connection between the causes, I would have to go through a whole series of relations with infinite ramifications. The only link between the events is the fact that _I am a witness_ to them all; mine are the eyes that see them. If I wanted to make a film about my walk through the city, all the unity and coherence would be a function of _my single perspective as a narrator._ (I might try to present a many-sided picture of the anonymity of the big city.) The structure of such a film would be _epic;_ the unity and the logic would be found on the _Plane of Discourse,_ in my point of view, my interpretations. It is not a dramatic unity.

So, then, some of the characteristics of _reality_ are as follows: it is apparently chaotic, full of coincidence, where everything that happens is linked to everything else in an unending and confused net, where causal connections are enormously complicated, where there is neither beginning nor end.

The relationships of reality can be illustrated like this:

Any attempt to make a whole with clearcut boundaries would be arbitrary. Everything touches everything else.

When we dramatize, we put a frame around a certain part of reality and establish clear relationships between the elements within this frame. It can be illustrated like this:

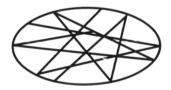

Certain elements of reality have been picked out and set in relationship to each other. Anything outside this pattern has been removed.

If my story of a day in Stockholm were to have a dramatic structure, I would have to establish relationships and inter-connections between the events on the _Plane of Events._ One of the people involved in the accident is perhaps the lover of the woman who quarrels with her husband and this is the cause of the quarrel. It turns out that my friend is not upset because he had to move to Stockholm but because he, too, has overheard the quarrel (without my knowing) and learned that the woman, whom he thought was _his_ mistress only, has another lover. He followed me to the cafe' in order to involve me in his plans . . .

So dramatization means giving *form* to chaos and coincidence so that the inter-connections between events appear *necessary and logical* and, above all, *clear and comprehensible* within the framework of a *defined dramatic space.*

Dramatic space is not the same thing as reality; it is a *concentrated and re-written* version of it. Within the framework of dramatic space, we have only included *those parts of reality that have a bearing on what we want to talk about,* and we have organized these parts in a way that gives us an *overview* and *control* over them.

We want dramatic space to *represent* and *clarify* reality in a way that we (and, we hope, the audience) find *reasonable,* but this does not mean that we simply *reflect* reality. Dramatic space is our *interpretation.*

Dramatic space is a *framework* that we use to present those aspects of reality that are essential *to us.* It is not a *mechanical reflection* of reality. It is rather a reflection of *our attitude* toward reality.

When we dramatize, we do so in order to make a *statement* about some aspect of reality that is important to us.

THE DRAMATIC LABORATORY MODEL

When we dramatize, we construct *dramatic situations* that oblige people to act in such a way that the *truth* about them comes out. We put people in situations where they must make decisive *choices* that they cannot avoid. The outcome of these choices brings out the truth.

The dramatic model can be likened to a scientist's laboratory experiment. For example, suppose a behavioral psychologist wants to study aggression in rats. He constructs a laboratory situation that enables him to *control* all of the factors which influence the rat's behavior. He then *varies* one of the conditions of the test (e.g., by subjecting the rat to electric shocks of varying strength) to see how the rat *reacts.* For example, if there are two rats in the cage that are normally compatible and they begin to fight as a result of the electric shocks the scientist can say something about the link between irritation and aggressive behavior. Schematically, it looks like this:

Manipulation (variation) of the experimental conditions (electric shocks). $\longrightarrow$	*Reactions* as a result of the manipulation (aggression).

By studying the relationship between his manipulations and the rat's reactions, the scientist tries to establish a scientific _law_.

In drama, we do not try to establish strict scientific laws but simply _human truths_. But the way in which we do this is very similar to the scientist's experimental method. We construct situations with built-in _conditions for conflict_ (manipulations) that instigate a _chain of events_ (reactions) that compel people to reveal their true selves. The outcome of the conflict contains the _premise_ of the drama—the human or artistic truth that we want to demonstrate. (The premise of the drama should be _discernible_ from the outcome; if anyone in the drama needs to _formulate_ it, this is often a sign that the construction is weak and implausible.) The premise in the drama is what the formulation of the law is to the scientist. Schematically:

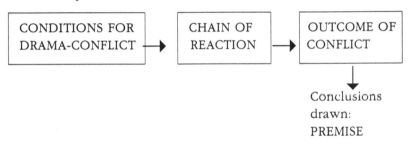

We can also liken the drama to a thunderstorm:

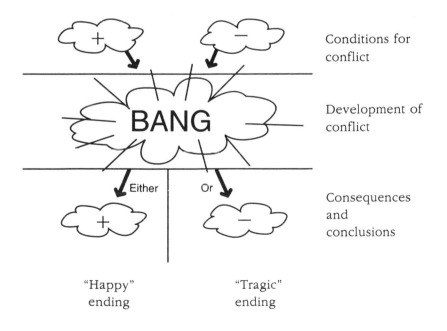

First, a state of *instability* is established. (1) Positively and negatively charged clouds approach each other. (2) The storm begins and the conflict is set in motion. (3) When the conflict (thunderstorm) reaches its climax, the tension between positive and negative forces is neutralized and either positive or negative clouds remain in the sky; i.e., the conflict has a desirable or undesirable outcome.

If we express the laboratory example and the thunderstorm example in terms of dramatic structure, we can illustrate it like this:

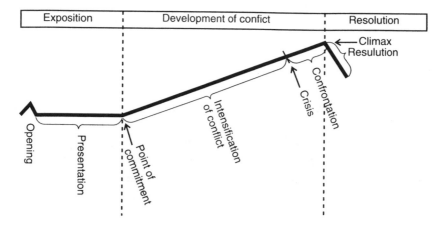

The *exposition* (opening and presentation) presents the conditions for the conflicts. The *point of commitment* is the point at which the balance is tilted to make the positive and negative forces react to each other, thereby instigating a *chain of reactions* that intensify to a *crisis point* (also called "point of no return," "black moment," "peripetia"), which makes a definitive *confrontation* inevitable. At the *climax*, the outcome of the confrontation is decided, and the *resolution* allows us to enjoy or cry over the new state of affairs.

At the point of commitment, the *dramatic aim* of the action is drawn up. This is the final point toward which the action steadfastly moves in order for the conflict to be resolved.

EXPOSITION

Since "dramatic space" is not a mechanical reflection of reality but rather a *simplification* that we make in order to have an overview and control over dramatic situations, we must tell the audience what our dramatic space looks like as well as explaining the "rules of the game" that apply within this space.

We can compare the drama with a game of chess. If the spectators do not understand the rules (how the various pieces can move, etc.), the game for them is just a series of incomprehensible movements. In the drama, the exposition explains these "rules of the game" and gives all the information necessary to enable us to follow the game with the greatest possible profit.

In the beginning, as far as the audience is concerned, dramatic space is like a large, empty stage. This stage space must be equipped in such a way that the conflicts and situations we create are able to work in a way the audience will understand. We must account for all the _conditions_ necessary for the development of the action. If the spectators do not have a complete understanding of these pre-conditions, the dramatic development will appear blurred and unclear and, therefore, uninteresting.

The exposition can be divided into _opening_ and _presentation_.

Opening

The main purpose of the opening is to arouse curiosity and interest and to make clear to the audience what sort of film they are about to see.

The first shots of the film are extremely important. They indicate the tone of the film and the direction we expect the drama to take. If the wrong expectations are created in the beginning, the whole film can be spoiled. We have to _hook_ the audience without giving too much away. At the same time we must not lead them astray.

One good way is to start _in medias res_, i.e., at a point in the story where a conflict is already unfolding. However, because the opening is an overture to the rest of the film, the material should be related to the _central conflict_. Films often open at the _point of commitment_, the point at which one or more people have to act in order to reach or avoid something that is important to them. It is then up to the presentation to supply information about anything important that may have happened before.

For the very reason that drama is an artificial construction with its own specific rules, we must bear in mind that whatever we introduce will set the terms for the subsequent development of the action. If we begin the film with the discovery of a murder in thriller style, the audience will feel duped if the rest of the film deals solely with the love life of a florist. In a work of art we expect to see an _organic relationship between part and whole_. If the film opens with

Woody Allen's slightly melancholy face telling a funny story (*Annie Hall*) we expect a film full of verbal humor and self-mocking irony, recounted in the unconventional Woody Allen *style*. If we make a promise that we do not later fulfill, we break an unspoken agreement. The audience has every right to have their expectations fulfilled; the challenge to the filmmaker is to fulfill them in an unexpected *way*!

Presentation

We normally treat the presentation, purely analytically, as that part of the film that furnishes detailed information regarding the conditions for the development of the dramatic action. It is vital that this information be given in such a way that the spectators do not feel that it is done for their sake. It is devastating if we feel that the characters are telling one another things they must know already (e.g., "Oh look, here comes your mother, who's been living alone since your father died last year and who had her kidney stones removed in the spring!"). Information should be integrated into situations where somebody has a natural interest in this information. In *One Flew Over the Cuckoo's Nest*, for example, we get all the relevant background information about McMurphy in the scene where Dr. Spivey interviews him. And the scene is completely natural and necessary in its context; this is what happens when somebody is admitted to a mental hospital. The scene is a textbook example of unobtrusive exposition; we do not think that its sole aim is to give us information; we are involved in the situation itself. Moreover, information should seldom, if ever, be given voluntarily. It is more dramatically effective when there is *resistance* and the character must be forced or enticed into disclosing information. Anything that is obvious at first glance is seldom of dramatic interest.

Above all, it is essential to present the following:

- Characters
- Relationships
- Settings
- Preconditions for conflict

We can regard dramatic space as a kind of *arena*, chosen to give the greatest opportunity for our conflicts to be expressed and developed. In this arena, we place the *characters*, who represent different sides and positions in the conflict. All the characters should have some kind of _relationship_ with one or more of the other characters, and we must be able to define this relationship as _positive or negative_ if it is to be dramatically viable. That is to say the second character is important in the context of what the first character is trying to attain or avoid. (In the positive sense, he can be the object or the means and in the negative sense he might constitute a threat or an obstacle.) The _settings_ (theaters of action) should be chosen so as to _produce conflict_ (e.g., the mental hospital as a formative space for the conflict between freedom and restraint). Once the characters have been presented, together with their relationships, objectives, interests, and affiliations and placed in settings where conflict naturally arises, the _preconditions for conflict_ must be clearly brought out. Only then can the dramatic situations begin to work.

One good way of controlling characters, relationships, and conditions for conflict is to draw a _diagram of relationships_. We can draw two arrows, one in each direction, for the different characters and state whether the second character represents something positive or negative to the first. If we take the presentation (the first flashback) in Carne's film _Le jour se lève_ as our example, we may draw the following diagram of relationships for the four important characters:

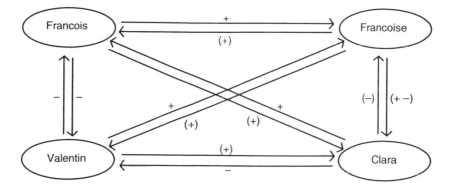

François wants Françoise, who is ambivalent because she is _also_ attracted to Valentin. Since Valentin also wants (to have power over) Françoise—a desire that is frustrated by Françoise being attracted to François—we put strongly negative arrows between François and Valentin. This negativity is further emphasized by the fact that Valentin's former lover, Clara, is strongly attracted to François, now that she has broken off with Valentin, whom she has since insulted in the supportive presence of François . . .

The diagram shows how the conditions for conflict have been formed by the emotional reinforcement of all the relationships. A final confrontation between François and Valentin seems inevitable.

It must be pointed out that anything that is presented must be relevant to the dramatic action. If something is emphasized in the presentation and is not later used, this is a serious fault. In drama, the *dramatic function* must always come first, and we should only present such matter as has a function in the dramatic fabric. Another way of saying this is that drama has a tacit agreement whereby everything that is presented *portends* something. The presentation as a whole functions as a *set-up* for subsequent dramatic exchanges (see "Set-up and Pay-off," in the next chapter).

(Things are quite different in the epic film, where the thematic function overshadows and sometimes replaces completely the dramatic function.)

If we want to bring the *thematics* of the film into the discussion, we can say that the exposition should imply the themes (main and secondary) without necessarily stating them overtly. The theme (e.g., blind ambition, its manifestation and consequences) should be embedded in the fabric of the drama through well-chosen characters who *develop* the theme through their involvement in the dramatic conflict. Schematically, it would look like this:

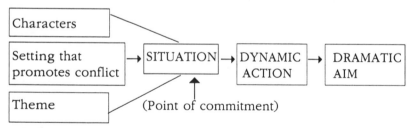

As a consequence of the dramatic tensions (conditions for conflict), the dramatic situation will set off a chain of events, propelling the action toward a dramatic aim (the resolution of the conflicts). At the point of commitment, *changes* in the situation are called for, compelling the characters to act in ways new to them. (This applies particularly to the protagonist, that person whose life is most thoroughly changed by his being involved in the drama.) The intensification of conflict can begin.

INTENSIFICATION OF CONFLICT: CONFRONTATION DYNAMICS

The beginning of the intensification of conflict is marked by someone's having to *act* because of his involvement in the conflict in order to change the situation. The objective of his action is what we here call the *dramatic aim*. The stimulus of his action is the point of commitment, i.e., something happens that means he can no longer be passive. If the dramatic aim is to fulfill its function in the drama, it must be *strongly motivated*. This could well mean that if the person does *not* achieve the dramatic aim, the consequences will be *disastrously negative*.

Example: A man's daughter has been kidnapped. Point of commitment: he is told that she will be killed if he does not come up with a certain sum of money by a certain time. Dramatic aim: to get the daughter back alive. The man now has several courses open to him: He can try to raise the money, or he can go to the police in the hope that they will be able to save his daughter, or he can try to dupe the kidnappers and save his daughter himself. He might even try all three, one after the other.

We may consider the intensification of conflict to be a series of *confrontations* on the person's route toward the dramatic aim. The person develops a series of *strategies*, each of which leads to confrontation. Each confrontation constitutes a new step toward the final solution. However, this does not necessarily mean that each confrontation *actually* takes him nearer the dramatic aim. They could just as easily be a gradual deterioration of his plight so that the dramatic aim seems more and more impossible to reach. But sooner or later, the person is pushed inexorably toward the final confrontation (the showdown).

Screenwriter Dwight Swain has outlined a model for the intensification of conflict that we shall follow. He calls it *confrontation dynamics*. This means a constant switching between *action* and *reaction*, or, as Swain puts it, confrontation and transition.

Confrontation is divided into three elements: *goal, conflict, and change of situation* (Swain calls this last part "catastrophe;" I choose a less drastic term because not every confrontation necessarily leads to a worse state of affairs.) The transition is divided into *reaction, dilemma and decision.*

Confrontation

Goal
In order to achieve the dramatic aim, the person must decide upon *preliminary aims*, which act as steps on the way. This aim represents the person's temporary intentions. It should be specific and concrete, strongly motivated (i.e., *necessary* from the person's own, subjective point of view—though, of course, he can turn out to have misjudged the situation), and within reasonable reach.

Conflict
The person's attempts to reach the objective are made difficult by *obstacles, complications, inner conflicts and/or counter-intentions*. Obstacle: something physical that is in the way (a closed door, a blocked road). Complication: some physical fault, either in the person or in his equipment or instruments (a broken arm, a car with no brakes, a broken transmitter). Inner conflict: a psychological weakness that causes the person to vacillate (fear of pain, fear of death, fear of heights). Counter-intention: one or more people who actively try to prevent the person from reaching his aim.

The meeting of the person with one or more of these difficulties leads to confrontation.

Change of situation
A new situation comes about as a result of the confrontation. This can be either better or worse than the preceding situation. The change in the situation is often *not foreseen* by the person concerned.

Transition

Reaction
The person reacts to the outcome of the confrontation in a *way* that is characteristic for him (e.g., he cries, gets drunk, runs fifteen times around the house, etc.) The reaction *shows* what the change in situation means to him. If he has not changed in any way (in attitude, understanding, involvement, readiness to act, and so forth) as a result of the confrontation, then the confrontation is probably a bad choice from a dramatic point of view. The conflict then remains static. (The function of the confrontations is above all to make the protagonist scale the ladder of development from 1 to 100. For more about this, see "Role Functions," in the next chapter.)

Dilemma
The person now has a *choice* of strategy or line of action. He has to evaluate new moments of danger, conditions, and possibilities as a result of the altered situation. *What* he chooses will show which consequences the confrontation has had for him.

Decision
The person chooses a *new strategy*, which then indicates the objective (the goal) of the next confrontation.

Not all dramatic works move toward a clearly defined dramatic objective in the way described here. The model is best suited to what might be called *action dramas* or goal-directed dramas where the dramatic aim is fairly clearly defined for the protagonist at the beginning of the intensification of the conflict. But in what we might call *reaction drama*, the protagonist is *faced with* a series of confrontations that he tries at length to *avoid*. He is gradually forced into becoming involved or taking a stand. However, in the end, he is faced with a *choice* that he cannot avoid; against his will, the conflict has become *his* conflict and he is compelled to act. He has reached the *crisis*, the *point of no return*.

Action drama versus reaction drama is also called *goal-directed drama* versus *character drama*. The character drama usually offers more space for psychological exploration.

CRISIS, CONFRONTATION AND CLIMAX

At the *crisis*, the drama has tightened so much that a final confrontation ("showdown") is inevitable. The protagonist has reached a point of no return, there is no way back. The action has taken a *dramatic turn* that forces him into the confrontation. (e.g., King Oedipus learns that he, himself, is the man he has promised to punish in order to save the city.) *How* he faces the confrontation will show who he truly is—he is compelled to learn the *truth* about himself (or, at least, if he refuses to see it, he must *reveal it to us* by his choice of action).

The *confrontation* often takes the form of a kind of *showdown* where all the cards are laid on the table, everything that has been concealed is revealed, and the naked truth comes out. ("Sit here, Torvald, we two have a lot to say to each other"—*A Doll's House*). At last the sub-text comes to the surface (see "Dialogue," chapter

11). People no longer grope around in the dark but make their choices from the depths of their inner selves.

In the *climax*, the protagonist finally comes to grips with his challenge; here it will be determined whether or not the dramatic objective is attained. Even if the protagonist does not reach the objective, through his action in the climax scene he can "cleanse" himself from a moral point of view (as when Macbeth meets his nemesis, Macduff, man-to-man).

The *outcome* of the confrontation and climax contains the premise (central idea) of the drama: Macbeth's ruthless ambition laid the foundations of his own ruin.

RESOLUTION

Not all dramas need a carefully worked out resolution. In Frankenheimer's *The French Connection II* the picture is frozen at the moment when Hackman's bullet hits the drug king between the eyes, whereas in Hitchcock's *Psycho*, a long explanation is necessary after the climax. The purpose of the resolution is often to give us the chance to give a sigh of relief or share in the joy of the protagonists (as they ride off together into the sunset) or in their grief (the camera backs slowly away from the hero, who lies dead on the ground).

As a rule, the resolution should be kept as short as possible. Who would want to ruin a tense dramatic experience with a tedious ending?

DRAMATIC STRUCTURE IN DOCUMENTARY AND FACTUAL PROGRAMS

In some cases, purely documentary events can take a dramatic course, and when this is the case, a conventional dramatic structure may be the best solution. This applies, for example, to Barbara Kopple's *Harlan County USA*, which is about a miner's strike. The preconditions of conflict must be presented, the parties identified. The intensification of conflict can later be followed through the confrontations to the final solution, and a "moral" (premise) can be drawn from the course of the events—seemingly from reality itself. Here the dramatic curve appears on the Plane of real Events. All that the shrewd and competent filmmaker has to do is bring it forth as forcibly as possible.

But, even in programs that do not follow a dramatic course of events but deal rather with the *clash of arguments*, the drama model can offer some help in structuring the program. Instead of dramatic characters, we have _interested parties_ who represent the different sides in a _conflict of interests or opinion._

For example: We want to make a film about pollutants. This is our _subject._

Let us say that our attitude toward pollutants can be formulated in the following _premise_ (central idea): The use of pollutants leads to the destruction of life and nature.

We choose an _opening_ (perhaps a provocative statement or a disturbing question) that focuses the problem in a way that makes the audience sit up and take notice.

We _present_ the problem, its background, and scope.

Then we let the respective parties present their cases.

Here, the intensification of conflict takes the form of an _argumentative intensification_, aiming at an effective focusing of the main question. In order to accomplish this, we must choose _concrete examples_ that support our chosen premise. (We must provide documentation, not just allegations.) We dig out any documentation that might prove that pollutants cause damage to life and to nature. This might be various forms of insecticide spraying, chemical fertilizers, water pollution, etc. We may then structure the program as follows: We _begin_ with the more inconclusive examples and _finish_ with the strongest, those that most incontrovertibly support our premise.

But what about the need for objectivity? We simply redefine it as a need for _pertinence_ and let the opponents present their argument. It is then up to us to prove them wrong by more convincing argument.

Intensification of conflict can then look something like this:

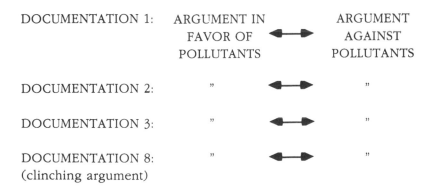

DOCUMENTATION 1: ARGUMENT IN FAVOR OF POLLUTANTS ◄—► ARGUMENT AGAINST POLLUTANTS

DOCUMENTATION 2: " ◄—► "

DOCUMENTATION 3: " ◄—► "

DOCUMENTATION 8: (clinching argument) " ◄—► "

CONCLUSIONS AND FINAL COMMENTS

In any case, it is we, the program-makers, who have all the advantages: we choose the pictures and decide the order of presentation, and we can always give ourselves the last word. (For example, we always give our opponent the chance to speak first, then we (or our allies) comment on (and correct) what the opponent has said. The person who speaks last always tends to have the stronger authority.)

We can also try to introduce a human-interest angle by giving the audience someone to *identify* with in the program. This should be someone who embodies, or has embodied, the questions asked by the program and who has come to the same conclusions as we have.

For example, we find a small farmer who has had to leave his land. Here is his story. The land did not yield enough for him and his family to live on. He heard of a new fertilizer that would triple the yield. The only drawback was that it had not been thoroughly tested and critics feared that, in the long run, it would cause disease in both animals and in crops. The farmer decided to give it a try.

Here we have something resembling a dramatic conflict. The aim: to stay on the farm. Complication: the means of doing this could turn out to be dangerous.

After a year or so, the crops began to change. The quantity rose but quality fell. The cattle became ill. The dog died and the farmer's wife began to show signs of sickness.

The family had to leave the farm for their health's sake. Their story, which can be reconstructed and integrated into the program, supports our thesis: The use of pollutants leads to the destruction of life.

14
Dramatic Elements

CONFLICT AND FORWARD MOVEMENT

In the literature of drama, we often read that all drama is based on *conflict*. Dramatic conflict might be further defined as a *conflict of will*.

A first pre-requisite for a dramatic situation is that somebody *desires* something. But this is not enough in itself. The person must be temporarily *unable* to obtain what he wants. The aim of his desire—what we might call the temporary dramatic aim—must be *difficult* to reach. (He is confronted by obstacles, complications, inner conflict and/or counter-intentions—see "Confrontation Dynamics" in the previous chapter.) Moreover, the person must be strongly motivated to achieve the objective, which means that he stands to lose a lot if he does not attain it. Failure to reach the objective may even mean catastrophe. (For instance, a man learns that if he is not in a certain place by a certain time, someone he loves will die.)

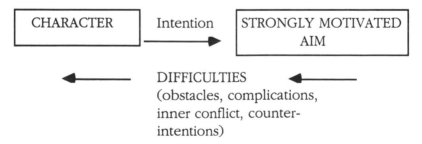

General rule: The *stronger the motivation* to reach the objective and the *more difficult* the objective is to reach, the greater the dramatic conflict.

Conflict creates *forward movement*. We want to know the outcome of the conflict, how the person is going to face the difficulties, what the counter-moves of his adversaries will be. Forward movement is the dynamic *motor* in the film. It should constantly make the audience wonder what is going to happen next.

One prerequisite of forward movement is *involvement*. If we are not interested in the characters in the film, we do not care what happens to them. So the drama needs one or more people that the audience will *identify* with. A way of creating identification that nearly always works is to put a character in an inferior position. Identification with the underdog would seem to be a very old and universal psychological mechanism. This does not mean, however, that the person should appear inferior in all circumstances. His inferiority should refer to the main conflict of the film, i.e., his thwarted desire to achieve the dramatic aim. The dramatic framework itself demands this. If the person were *not* in an inferior position, he would resolve the conflict at once, and where there is no conflict, there is no drama. The dramatic aim has been reached and the film is over.

In general, we can say that the greater the inferiority of the protagonist and the greater the superiority of those who represent the difficulties he must overcome, the stronger the dramatic circumstances. The person has as *long and hard a road to travel as possible*. This brings about a whole series of situations and confrontations. Curiosity and uncertainty are maintained as regards how he will face the confrontations. Forward movement is kept up.

Forward movement can also be created by means of a *dramatic question* to which the protagonist must find the answer before he can resolve the conflict (e.g., "Who is the murderer?" "Why have the children disappeared?"). The conflict here lies in the very difficulty in obtaining information.

We can also create forward movement by *foreshadowing* conflict. We are told that something is going to happen but not how, why, when. It is important not to give too much away here. When the thing happens it should come as a surprise.

However, it is sometimes advisable to give the audience a chance to *guess or assume* what is going to happen and to later give them the satisfaction of knowing they were right. But they must not be allowed to guess everything. There must be unforeseen elements in the solution. When everything is obvious and predictable, nothing is exciting.

The conflict matter in a film should always be organized around a central _main conflict_. This conflict is a concrete translation into action of the main theme of the film (e.g., duty versus love). The main conflict may be supported by one or more _secondary conflicts_, which must be thematically related to the main theme. Solving the secondary conflicts should lead us toward the solution of the main conflict; they may be necessary detours on the way toward the eventual dramatic aim. Secondary conflicts make for variation and enable things to be seen from different angles.

Great care must be taken to avoid three errors when working with conflict material:

1) _"Hopping" conflict_: The phases of development of the conflict are insufficiently prepared. A person jumps from condition A to condition B without this change being mediated through a confrontation and a subsequent change of situation that make us understand the change.

2) _"Static" conflict_: The conflict causes no change to anyone. People find themselves in the same situation all the time. Relationships, attitudes, readiness to act, etc., are not affected. Things remain in the end as they were in the beginning. (This, of course, might be the whole _point_, but if this is the case, we have to see how the characters _fail_ despite their efforts to change things.)

3) _"Blurred" conflict_: The persons' intentions are not made clear. We do not know what they want or what they are fighting for. If we want to have contradictory and ambivalent characters, we cannot have them on _both_ sides of the conflict or the scene loses its direction and dramatic drive.

DRAMATIC PROGRESSION: ACTION AND REACTION

Dramatic progression—the spectator's feeling that tension is steadily being increased—is created by the gradual and inexorable tightening of the dramatic circumstances to the point where all the tensions have to be released. Between the chains of events is a close cause-and-effect relationship by which every scene occurs as a consequence of the scenes that precede it and _conditions_ those that follow. While the drama can be set in motion by a series of *coincidences*, the dramatic resolution is reached by *necessity*. Between these extremes, events move—between the point of commitment and the crisis—in a framework of *probabilities*, leading step by step to the necessity of the final confrontation.

Dramatic progression means that every action leads to *change* (however small). If there is no change, the drama stands still. (In certain cases, however, the whole *point* is that nothing changes.) At first, the changes can be quite small but grow more profound as the crisis approaches. The changes (in attitude, readiness to act, behavior, etc.) come about as a result of what people are exposed to, how they act and react. In simple terms, we might say that dramatic progression is created by the interchange between *action and reaction*.

As a general rule, we shall say here that *an action has no dramatic meaning until someone has reacted to it*. (Many so-called "action films" are completely undramatic for this reason—we never have the chance to see what the events *mean* to those involved, the confrontations are superficial and, in the long run, uninteresting and tedious—e.g., the James Bond film *Octopussy*).

The smallest dramatic unit in a dramatic work always consists of the two elements action and reaction. For instance, a man is sitting alone in his flat; he cannot concentrate, he is waiting for something to happen. Suddenly the telephone rings, he rushes over to it and picks up the receiver. He listens. Then he puts the receiver down slowly, staring into space. A few seconds later he breaks down in tears. The dramatic condition: waiting for something to happen. Action: picking up the phone and listening. Reaction: despair and tears. We actually do not yet need to know what has happened—the dramatic unit lies in the combination of action and reaction *as such*. Whatever was said on the telephone *assumes* importance because of the man's reaction.

In films, this "smallest dramatic unit" is usually given form by the use of *reaction shots*. If we look at a film like Forman's *One Flew Over the Cuckoo's Nest*, we will see that the dramatic tension is produced by the number of reaction shots and their *timing*. *Nothing* happens that does not acquire significance and weight through somebody's reaction.

However, the reaction to an event does not need to follow immediately on the heels of the event itself (it does not even need to occur in the same scene). *Delayed* reaction is a well-tried dramatic technique. But sooner or later the reaction must come or the action has no dramatic function.

EMPATHY

Involving the audience means maintaining their _interest_ in the development of the dramatic action. Empathy reinforces audience involvement in the conflicts and, above all, reinforces their _identifying_ with the characters.

In some dramatic models, the creation of empathy is emphasized at a specific point in the dramatic structure. This occurs between the presentation and the beginning of the intensification of conflict. The reason behind this is that, since the presentation is there primarily to give information, we need a subsequent reinforcement of the audience's emotional identification with the "right" characters before the conflict gets properly under way.

Of course, it _can_ be done this way. But it is just as common, and more effective, to shape the situations of the presentation in such a way that empathy is constantly secured. In order for empathy to build up, we must create characters that are experienced by the audience as three-dimensional people of flesh and blood as opposed to cardboard stereotypes. The French director Renoir once said, "Everybody has a reason for doing what he does," by which he meant that it is our task to show that even the most unlikable persons act as they do because of their background, their situation, and their nature. We must _understand_ them, _feel with them_ as people—even though they are playing the part of the "bad guy." Only then does the drama acquire depth.

Finding universal points of contact between the struggles of the characters and the audience's own situation, their fears, dreams, and hopes is a good way of establishing empathy. The audience then finds it easy to enter into the world of the fictional people. The conflicts acquire the necessary space for resonance in the audience's own feelings and experiences.

Empathy should run through the whole course of the drama. Every transition from one confrontation to another should deepen our involvement in the drama, showing us new aspects of the characters and increasing our understanding of them. This is really the purpose of the transition: to bind us emotionally to the characters, to make their dilemma our dilemma.

SET-UP AND PAY-OFF

Anything that is presented in the drama should have a *function* in the dramatic development. When we introduce people or things in a dramatic framework, we always do so with the intention of *making use of them later.* The more we emphasize or underline something in the beginning, the more important a part it will have during the development of the conflicts. This is a *tacit agreement* we have with the audience; when we present something, we sow the *expectation* that it will be of significance at a later stage. If something that is presented turns out not to have any function, the audience will wonder why we put it there in the first place; they will feel misled. This is because of the deliberate exclusivity of dramatic space; drama is deliberately *selective* and anything that is not necessary to the dramatic action has been (or should have been) removed.

We *set out the pieces on the board,* so to speak. These pieces will become the tools of the drama. Technically, this is known as *setting up.* Expressed figuratively: In the beginning we plant the seeds of the tree that the hero will later climb in order to save his life.

The later effect of the set-up is called the *pay-off.*

Schematically:

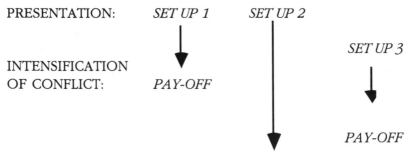

PRESENTATION:	*SET UP 1*	*SET UP 2*	
			SET UP 3
INTENSIFICATION OF CONFLICT:	*PAY-OFF*		
			PAY-OFF
CLIMAX		*PAY-OFF*	

Setting up means *charging objects, behavior, personal qualities, etc., with dramatic significance.* Generally speaking, anything can be charged in this way. All we have to do is show that it means something to one or more of the characters. If, toward the end of the film, the dramatic release turns out not to work as planned, the reason is nearly always that it was not set up properly to begin with.

Example: In _One Flew Over the Cuckoo's Nest_ we have a tremendous dramatic pay-off when Chief lifts up the water fountain and throws it through the window. This scene would never have acquired its dramatic effect if the significance of the water fountain had not been set up in the scene where McMurphy _tries_ to lift the fountain and fails. The fountain is dramatically charged and will later symbolize the effort to break out into freedom. The fountain _retains_ this charge until it has fulfilled its purpose.

ROLE FUNCTIONS

Role functions must not be confused with character attributes. Role functions simply indicate the placing of the characters in the dramatic network. A given character can have more than one role function at the same time or change role functions during the course of the film. The role functions are wholly determined by the _plot_ of the film (the web of interdependent events that lead to the climax, i.e., the progression of events brought about by the constant interchange of cause and effect).

To a considerable extent, the role functions determine which attributes the characters can have in order to function in the dramatic context. (A self-assured, well-adjusted person could not serve as the protagonist in _Taxi Driver_, only a person of infinite ambition and with the need to be liked could be the protagonist in _Citizen Kane._)

We can identify a number of role functions that occur in most dramatic works.

1. THE PROTAGONIST (PRINCIPAL ROLE)

The protagonist is the one who, by his involvement in the drama, undergoes the _greatest development and change._ In our dramatic laboratory analogy, he is the test animal that the experimenter causes to act and react by modifying the test conditions (conditions for conflict in drama). In his development, he acts out or _sustains the premise of the film_, i.e., it is he who _demonstrates_ the development that lies in the statement "X leads to Y." For example, if we want to show that poverty leads to crime, the protagonist cannot already be a criminal at the beginning of the film; he must be forced by circumstances to _become_ a criminal. He might, for example, be an honest citizen who suddenly finds himself without a penny to his name. We show how the new circumstances push him gradually into crime. Like this:

Manipulations:	**Reactions:**	
Conditions for conflict: Poverty, unemployment, loss of friends, etc.	Reactions and actions leading toward crime	Consequences: Criminal behavior

In order to illustrate this development as cogently as possible, the protagonist should, at the beginning, be as far as possible from his eventual plight. We must, therefore, establish the *poles* of his development. For example, if we say that the premise in *Citizen Kane* is that the ruthless lust for power leads to loneliness, we must, at the beginning, find the *antipole* to Kane's loneliness. We show that Kane is loved by everybody (the scene where he is feted by his employees). Because of his ruthless quest for power, Kane drives himself further and further into loneliness and isolation. His development can be traced on a scale where 1 is the starting point and 100 the point that he reaches in the end.

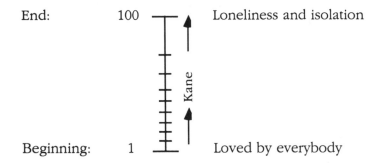

End: 100 — Loneliness and isolation

Beginning: 1 — Loved by everybody

The various situations and confrontations that Kane causes or undergoes in the course of the film show how he gradually *climbs the ladder*, how, increasingly, he loses friends, support, and love. Every change of situation (points on the scale) must be motivated by confrontation and choices of action that cause the change. The steps are often small in the beginning, leading gradually to stronger confrontations and greater change.

The principal role must not start *from scratch*. The *preconditions* must exist for him to progress from one pole to the other. There should be some character attribute (often concealed or even unknown to the person himself) that indicates the direction in which the character will develop. Because of his attributes and the situation he is in, the protagonist should already have reached a point where he is *ripe for a change*. The dramatic process of change, then, begins at the "point of commitment."

2. THE ANTAGONIST (OPPONENT)

The antagonist is the role figure (or figures) who gets the dramatic course of events under way, thereby compelling the protagonist to act. Even if this driving force is the environment itself, it should be made concrete and specific and, if necessary, embodied in one or more characters who *represent* the environment. It is never a good idea to let the antagonist be abstract or too general. Although we may seldom, if ever, see him, he should be potentially visible; he *can* pop up in any place at any time (e.g., the monster in the science-fiction film *Alien*).

The antagonist need not, of course, be a human being; it may be, for example, an animal (*Jaws*) or forces of nature.

The *strength* of the antagonist (the threat he represents) generally remains *constant* throughout the film. The antagonist does not develop, he remains at 100 all the time. (If he were weakened, the temperature of the drama would drop immediately.)

It is important that the antagonist should act *out of necessity* (e.g., getting what he wants is a matter of life and death to him). Often the climax of the drama is a definitive and inevitable confrontation between protagonist and antagonist.

3. THE ASSISTANT OR HELPER

If the film has a helping character, he is often the evenly matched opponent of the antagonist. He wants the exact opposite of what the antagonist wants and should be just as strongly motivated to get what he wants.

The function of the assistant in drama is often to *keep the conflict going* until the protagonist is able to or chooses to or is compelled to intervene. Then the assistant's part is often taken over by the protagonist. (In *One Flew Over the Cuckoo's Nest*, for example, it is McMurphy who keeps up the struggle against Nurse Ratched—the antagonist. Only when McMurphy has been rendered harmless does Chief—the protagonist—take the independent step toward freedom.)

Any struggle between the antagonist and the assistant serves to prepare the ground for the development of the protagonist, his progress from 1 to 100 in terms of the conflict.

The assistant role does not develop during the film—he, too, is always at 100.

(The assistant or helper is often considered, by the general public, to be the protagonist, but this is not the case in dramaturgical terms.)

4. SHADOW ROLES

Shadow roles help to illuminate and define the development that the protagonist undergoes. Their development, which is *like* that of the principal role though less radical (they do not climb as far up the ladder), forms variations and support for the premise that is the basis of the development of the protagonist. (E.g., poverty leads to crime: a good friend is arrested for a minor offence. His fate portends what *might* happen to the protagonist.)

Shadow roles are often drawn with less detail than the principal role but they, too, must appear to be people of flesh and blood. Characters must never be *reduced* to their role functions.

5. CONTRAST ROLES

Contrast roles are involved in the conflicts in the same way as shadow roles, but their development *contrasts* with the development of the protagonist. They develop in the opposite direction and, as a result, put the development of the protagonist into relief (often tragic relief: they illustrate the circumstances that *might* have caused the protagonist to *choose differently*).

6. THE SYMPATHIZER

The sympathizer acts as an intimate, confidential ally of the protagonist or some other character. He listens to what the other says, asks and answers questions, etc., which help the other person to *open out*. By his reactions, the sympathizer helps to clarify the protagonist's situation. Sometimes this role is a caricature (e.g., Robin Hood's right-hand-man, Little John).

7. THE PROXY

The proxy is a spectator figure who does not intervene personally in the conflicts. It is often the proxy who leads the audience into the action. He observes and asks questions *on behalf of* the audience. He is the man in the street who reacts more or less as we ourselves would react. (In Costa-Gavras' films, the proxy is nearly always a journalist—*Z, State of Siege.*)

8. THE "FIVE-MINUTE PART"

A role that gives pause for breath and often comic relief. It often acts as a distorting mirror for the action.

15
EPIC STRUCTURE

EPIC VERSUS DRAMATIC STRUCTURE

A modern dictionary defines *drama* as "that branch of literary art in which the writer speaks indirectly, through characters who are brought to the stage to talk, act and decide; in contrast to the lyric, whose message is of a more subjective nature, or to the epic and the novel, where the narrative element, the descriptive representation of the inner lives of the characters, or of external events, plays an essential part . . . Drama depicts principally a circumscribed complex of intentions that mutually influence one another."

In terms of this definition, when something is dramatized, an *illusion* is made of the situation that is to be presented, by someone *acting it out* as if it were taking place there and then. In one word, this type of representation can be called *scenic*.

The epic situation, however, is one that is *reported* by one person to another.

For example, if we want to tell someone about a funny person we have met, we can either try to give a pictorial *description* of the person (epic representation) or try to *imitate* the person's movements and gestures (dramatic representation).

Drama recreates events in the form of concrete *action*, the epic reports events by *describing* them.

There is no *necessary* opposition between the dramatic and the epic. They offer, however, quite different possibilities in form and structure.

One theorist who has tried most systematically to distinguish between dramatic and epic form is Berthold Brecht. He arranges things like this:

Dramatic Form	Epic Form
action	narrative
involves the spectator in the action	invites the spectator to observe, but
destroys his readiness to act	arouses his readiness to act
gives him a sensation	compels him to make decisions
experience	conception of the world
the spectator is involved in something	the spectator is confronted with something
suggestion	argument
instinctive feelings preserved	is brought to understanding
the spectator is in the midst of events, shares the experience	the spectator stands outside and observes
human nature is a known entity	human behavior is examined
mankind is unchangeable	mankind is changeable and can bring about change
the excitement lies in how things will turn out in the end	the excitement is in the action itself
one scene leads to another self	each scene is complete in it-self
growth	montage
linear development	curved development
evolutionary determinism	progress in leaps
mankind is constant	mankind as a process
thought determines being	social being determines thought
emotion	reason

Many of these distictions, with varying degrees of emphasis, will be found in the examination that follows.

THE DISINTEGRATION OF DRAMATIC SPACE

Drama portrays a world. We might say that it gives us a concentrated picture that _represents_ the world. In the center are thinking, active people. They are the movable pieces on the board and stand in well-defined and visible relationships to one another. From one event to the next there is a clear connection of cause and effect that moves the action in a determined direction: toward the resolution of the dramatic conflicts. The drama _isolates_ these relationships, selecting and showing only what influences and is influenced by the dramatic course of events. Anything that is not part of this _circumscribed whole_ has been rejected.

In other words, the unity of drama takes shape on the _Plane of Events_ itself. The forces that are released on the Plane of Events must be able to explain everything that happens or we are left with gaping holes in the dramatic tissue. The _dramatic function_ is fundamental in selection and structuring; the tensions in the supposed reality that is conjured up must seem themselves to decide what the audience is going to see. _The Plane of Discourse is therefore subordinate to the Plane of Events._

The genuine dramatic film, then, has a _form_ that brings out the dramatic events in such a way that the audience feels involved in the supposed reality of the situation. The audience should be enveloped in this, "forgetting" for the moment that they are seeing a film. This effect is referred to as the "suspension of disbelief"; if people do not _believe_ in the film, even though they know it is "only a film," it loses its dramatic power of conviction. The dramatic events should attract all our attention—we should see things as if we were really present and able to choose the best vantage point. The _way_ in which we are shown the action—i.e., all the narrative devices of the Plane of Discourse—must be unnoticed. We have to forget that there is somebody behind it, deciding what we are going to see and _how_ we are going to see it. For this reason, the genuine dramatic film tries to find a _form_ that makes the director's intervention "invisible." We should not notice the cutting, we should not notice how time is compressed and how vantage points change. We should simply be carried along, absorbed by the apparent reality of the film.

In this type of film, the writer/filmmaker is a kind of god; he has created his own picture of the world, dramatic space. He sees and knows everything in it. The creator of a classical drama must, therefore, be able to answer any questions that concern his characters. It is *presumed* that he has insight and control of all the elements in the representation of the reality that he has made. He decides and controls the conditions in his dramatic "laboratory experiment" to such an extent that the characters can only behave as they do and in no other way. They scurry around in his hands like the mice in the psychiatrist's electrical maze.

What distinguishes a dramatic character from a real-life character is the fact that he acts according to *preconditions imposed by us* (personal attributes, social relations, needs, intentions, etc.), conditions that we decide and define. In real life we never know why people act as they do; we can only guess, leaving a wide margin for doubt (this applies even when we ourselves are the subject of study). We never know anyone completely, not even a person we have spent a lifetime with. Everyone has a hidden core. Moreover, it is impossible to have a complete overview of human relations, and human relations owe so much to chance. We cannot assert with complete confidence that a person commits action B because another person committed action A. We can only guess. If we ask the person, he may confirm our guess, but how do we know he is not lying?

In real life, all the classical criteria of drama are invalidated: "complete" characters, controllable situations, relations of which we have an overall view, necessary and logical development of action, clear relations of cause and effect, dramatic intensification. We lose almost everything that creates unity and coherence on the Plane of Events in drama.

In schematic form, the difference between drama and real life might be roughly:

Drama	*Real life*
Everything under control	Nothing under control
The writer/filmmaker determines the development of action according to rules and conditions imposed by him	The development of action is determined by an endless jumble of causes and conditions
Action is logical and necessary	Action is casual and irregular
Reality is known	Reality is unknown

Let us say we want to make a film that represents real life or captures it in its infinite multiplicity. The first thing to do is to destroy the well-ordered, well-defined structure of dramatic space. Relationships on the Plane of Events are no longer the clear, logical whole that we can take for granted but themselves become the object of study. We no longer know more about the people than what we can see—they are there in all the complexity of their make-up. Real life keeps its secrets; we no longer look for the Answer but search around among many possible answers.

When the Plane of Events—"reality"—no longer constitutes a circumscribed and controllable whole, this does not necessarily mean that the _film_ we make will not have coherence and structure. _The unity that, in the dramatic film, was formed on the Plane of Events must now be created on the Plane of Discourse._

CHARACTERISTICS OF THE PLANE OF DISCOURSE IN THE EPIC FILM

Even the genuine dramatic film is narrated by _somebody_: every camera angle, every sequence of shots constitutes a creative _choice_, which means that somebody is interpreting and guiding the narrative. But what is typical in this sort of film is the fact that the storyteller makes himself as _invisible_ as possible; as an audience, we should not notice that he is there pulling the strings. He has, so to speak, _hidden behind the characters_ he has created. His narrative style submits to and strengthens the action on the Plane of Events and reduces to a minimum the distance between it and the Plane of Discourse. On the face of it, it is the fictitious reality itself that tells the story, not the narrator.

If, however, the filmmaker wants to portray a situation that is _not_ known and where the relationships on the Plane of Events do not form a logical, well-defined whole, how can he set about it? What can he do to prevent the various parts of the narrative from falling away from each other, leaving a casually assembled mosaic with no recognizable direction, unity, or coherence?

Let us say that three people, A, B, and C, have no discernible relation to each other. We only have partial knowledge of them, and the information we have about them is contradictory and possibly misleading. Can we, in spite of this, make a film about them?

If we decide that the Plane of Events should retain the complexity and many-sidedness of reality, structure and coherence must be created on the *Plane of Discourse*. This means that we, *as narrators*, make ourselves visible as observers and interpreters of what is shown on the Plane of Events. And, above all, this distinguishes the epic form; it presumes, and lets the audience understand, that what is being recounted is being looked at *from a particular point of view*. It is selected and recounted by *somebody* who directly or indirectly admits his presence. There is not necessarily any connection between the events he selects—the narrator simply finds them interesting from a particular point of view. This point of view is his narrative vantage point. The narrative vantage point—the filmmaker's *way of seeing things*—will give the film its unity. The study he makes of things must be coherent and consistent, even if what he is studying is not.

The epic perspective emphasizes the fact that what we see is the narrator's way of looking at things—one *among many possible*. Another narrator would see the same events in a different way, apply other interpretations, and draw completely different conclusions—even when he points his camera at the same situations. The epic relation to real life means exactly that—there is no "reality as such." And if this is so, we can no longer pretend that a story taken from real life can be formed and developed irrespective of who the narrator is.

In films where the narrator openly comes out and organizes the story, we may say that the Plane of Events submits to the Plane of Discourse. As spectators, we are aware of the narrator as a *mediator* between reality per se and the filmed version of reality. He is a link who marks reality with his particular way of seeing it; we are reminded that we see things through *his* eyes. This invites the spectator to maintain a reflective distance (in some cases a critical distance) from what is shown on the Plane of Events—a distance that allows both empathy and analysis at the same time.

This has decisive *dramaturgical* consequences. The logic of classical drama can be dispensed with. The epic distancing means that we observe the Plane of Events obliquely, from the outside; it becomes an object of study. It is no longer the relationships between the characters that give the film its direction and unity. The Plane of Events can be cut up, turned over or inside out, precisely as the filmmaker wants. The characters can be as fleeting and diffuse as they are in real life, their intentions can turn out to be only of minor significance. The dramatic "tissue" on the Plane of

Events can be full of "holes," the events themselves can be without beginning or end, motivations obscure, events unexplained and with no visible connection to one another.

Since, naturally, we do not want the _film_ to be chaotic and incoherent, _the direction and unity, which in classic drama were on the Plane of Events, must now be transposed to the Plane of Discourse_. The overall perspective from which the actual epic examination is made must guarantee the unity and the integrity of the film. The filmmaker's point of view and his thematic _leitmotifs_ must be consistent and create interest. He can choose to recount anything he likes and (within the limits for normal comprehension and coherence) put his story together in any way he likes as long as it is held together by the unity of his narrative _approach_ to the subject he has chosen.

Whereas classical drama has a "premise" as its driving force (it shows that certain conditions lead to certain consequences—X leads to Y), the epic work is held together by a _main theme_, which is formed and developed from a consistent narrative point of view. For example, if the theme is crime, the Plane of Events can consist of a series of episodes and occurrences that never touch each other (there is no cause-and-effect relationship; perhaps the events happen in different places at different times). What they have in common is that they all exemplify and form variations on the _theme_ of crime. The filmmaker's point of view—his questions, clarifications, interpretations, and comments (elements of the Plane of Discourse!) must form the overall perspective, which assembles all the parts to make the whole.

In drama, it is man himself who brings the truth out into the open; in the epic this is done by the examining eye of the narrator. Drama _demonstrates_ (acts out) the truth; the epic brings it out or surmises it—as far as it goes. The epic examination can also emerge in a dramatic premise, but this is not necessarily the case. Much more frequently, the epic _questions_ simple dramatic premises, such as "true love conquers death"—are we so sure about that? One of the great merits of the epic film is its capacity to raise questions, to bring out the known and the less known in an unexpected light and reveal new secrets.

We may illustrate the difference between dramatic and epic structure by making two patterns of bricks. For the drama, we arrange the bricks like this:

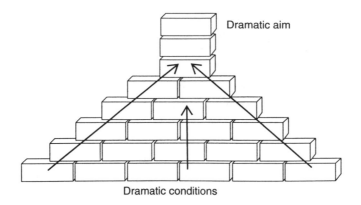

Dramatic aim

Dramatic conditions

The arrows in the drawing represent the direction of movement of the drama. Each row of bricks (which are piled upon each other) represents a stage in the development of the dramatic conflict. Each row *presupposes* the row below it, and there is a gradual tightening up all the way to the last brick: the dramatic aim. So the dramatic aim can only be reached by building the pyramid row by row.

In an epic structure, the bricks can be arranged like this:

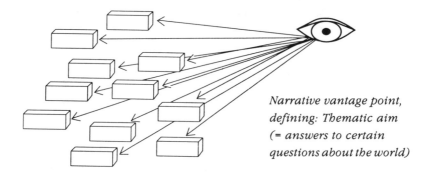

Narrative vantage point,
defining: Thematic aim
(= answers to certain
questions about the world)

Here, we arrange all the bricks on a table and look at them from above. Each brick represents a segment of reality, which illustrates and illuminates the theme we are studying. But they are not inter-dependent; any of them can be removed without this affecting the others. From our chosen point of view (vantage point), however, the various bricks might form a *pattern* that only becomes clear when we have studied each brick individually. It matters less in that order we look at the bricks (variations on the theme); the main thing is that we see them all so clearly that the pattern emerges in the end. The order we actually choose depends on the logic and progression of the epic examination itself.

We have spoken here about epic and drama as pure structures, ideal types. However, it seldom happens that a film is *wholly* dramatic or *wholly* epic. Every possible combination exists. However, they cannot be combined indiscriminately, and so it is important to identify the dramatic and epic characteristics in an analytical way to know how and under which conditions we can combine them.

THE EPIC BIOGRAPHY

Perhaps the simplest form of epic construction is the one that takes us through a course of events from beginning to end, though without forcing events to take a rigid, dramatic turn. We try to be as faithful as possible to the truth in portraying the changes and quirks of fate that affect human life. Situations follow one another with nothing to connect them on the Plane of Events but the *chronology*. Every scene stands on its own and is not—as it is in the drama—the inevitable consequence of what goes before it. (Whereas the drama says "First A, *therefore* B," the epic says simply "First A, *then* B.") We can be relating anything from the simple story of a person's life to an entire historical era. The era is often depicted through the lives of one or more people during which its various phases are reflected—Bertollucci's *1900* (about Fascism in Italy), John Ford's *Cheyenne Autumn* (about the struggle of the Cheyenne Indians for their homelands), or Troell's *Emigrants* films.

But it is often the individual human destiny itself that is at the center, while the external historical and social circumstances act as a sounding board or background color to the human endeavor that recurs in all ages. (Some good examples of such films are *Petrija*, by the Yugoslav Karanovic, Fassbinder's *Effi Briest*, Kubrick's *Barry Lyndon* and, of course, Troell's *Here's Your Life*.)

Films that follow an individual destiny, a family story, or an era are often structured around the beginning and the end of large or small events: a person is born, a person dies—an era opens and closes. Between the two extremities we register all the changes and important events that give spice and flavor to that particular life or that particular era.

Naturally, in this type of film, too, a careful selection must be made from the vast amount of material that goes to make up a human life or a whole era. But the selection is not made chiefly for *dramatic* reasons but rather for *thematic* reasons. While the drama is bound together by a premise (which provides the story with its necessary and logical development), the epic narrative is held together by a *main theme* (sometimes with related secondary themes). We cannot say *everything* about a person but focus our attention instead on *some aspect* of the person that interests us. Truffaut's *Jules et Jim*, as the title suggests, is a film about two men. It is a story that shoots off without the least respect for the rules of drama; we are flung, to all appearances spontaneously and unexpectedly, from one situation to another. But this is not arbitrary selection. Every scene or episode throws new light on, and gives us a deeper insight into, the film's unifying theme: the *friendship* between Jules and Jim. The film begins with their first meeting and ends when one of them dies. Between these two chronological extremes we see how their friendship is subjected to the most arduous strains and provocations, from war to rivalry in love. The effect of such an epic presentation is *cumulative*, it is put together piece by piece until eventually we have a *mosaic* of situations and events whose overall effect is to give a many-faceted picture of the theme of the film: friendship. (Another great film that treats the condition of friendship in a similar way is Kurasawa's *Dersu Uzala*.)

There is no reason why this sort of epic story should not be divided up into a certain number of episodes, each one having a dramatic build-up. This is done, for example, in *1900* and *Dersu Uzala*. But the individual episodes must be subordinated to the overall epic perspective and its thematic direction or the film will fall apart. Moreover, epic and drama must be blended in a consistent *manner*. It is not wise to do what Widerberg does in *Joe Hill*, where the first two-thirds follows the loose logic of epic biography and the last third is a tight drama. Laila Mikkelsen falls into the same trap in *Little Ida* when she starts by constructing a situation full of dramatic conditions and then goes into an epic narrative.

THE EPIC JOURNEY

While the epic biography dissolves the strict dramatic logic as far as time is concerned, the epic journey breaks down the tight construction of dramatic _space_. Settings have not necessarily been isolated and concentrated to give the maximum formative space for a central conflict but rather follow on from one another with a logic that, from a dramatic point of view, is as random as the changes in the landscape. The constant changes in setting actually counteract any tendency toward a steady dramatic intensification. While drama is characterized by logical _development_, we could say that the epic journey is marked by random _change_. The person or persons we follow on the journey may not develop at all, but each new place they come to reveals new facets of them. The settings are used to throw their traits of character into relief so that, as an audience, we are given new information and insight into how these people face up to the challenges and varying fortunes of life. These people are often running away _from_ something or looking _for_ something. The new places they frequently come to often reflect changes in their own psychology. For this reason, the journey is often a kind of _metaphor_ for the search for identity (as in Antonioni's _The Outcry, The Adventure, Zabriskie Point_, and _The Passenger_). "Road movies" such as _Easy Rider_ and _Radio On_ often work in a similar way.

Even though changes of place can appear random, the way in which they are selected and used in the film is not immaterial. A _thematic direction_ should be the basis for geographical shifts (e.g., in the search for identity as mentioned above). Every new place then forms a new _variation_ on the main theme and if, in the end, the person or persons go back to their starting point (as in Antonioni's _The Outcry_), we see things in a wholly different way. Just as in music, the variations _enhance_ our perception of the main theme.

The journey often acts as a framework in stories where people from completely different backgrounds are _thrown together_ and compelled to co-exist for a certain period of time. Different stages on the way bring about changes in the enforced relationships, falsity is revealed, and characters are exposed (in the Yugoslav film _Who's Singing Over There?_ for example). Of course the journey motif can be combined with a tight dramatic structure (the bus, the boat, or the plane becomes a sort of controlled laboratory situation), but the dramatic logic may in other cases be of quite minor significance (as in Fellini's *And the Ship Sails On*; Coppola's *Apocalypse Now* falls somewhere between these two extremes).

In some cases, places are not used to throw light on people but it is the people who direct our attention toward changes and shifts in the *places*. The people travelling are simply tools used, for example, to show the stages in political and sociological development. As characters, these people may not be of much interest, their most important job is to direct our eyes to the ambiguities and complexities of reality. For example, Angelopoulos' *The Travelling Players* allows us to experience a whole era of Greek history with a group of travelling actors.

We often see that epic biography is combined with the journey motif. Good examples of this are Troell's *The Emigrants* and Kubrick's *Barry Lyndon* as well as Ford's *Cheyenne Autumn*.

THE STATE-OF-MIND FILM

Drama in the classical sense is based on dynamic forces that are set in *motion*. Without motion, there is no drama. The moment, in that case, is no longer imbued with the demand or expectation of new action but remains static. Progression—the dynamic motor in the development of action—has ceased to operate and we no longer wonder what is going to happen next.

In drama, we must always stimulate forward movement; if it stops, the drama loses its force. The moment has no value in itself but is only a step on the way to the objective: the resolution of conflict.

This is not the case in all narrative. The purpose of narrative need not be to carry us forward; on the contrary, it can be to make us stop and think about how things are in a given situation. Really think, observe, listen, and reflect. *Ingression or inward movement* might be more appropriate terms here than progression or forward movement. The moment, in this case, is a central point around which thoughts, associations, observations, and reflections revolve. This implies a wholly different attitude toward the phenomena of reality. Reality itself becomes a source of meditation and curiosity, a puzzle to be penetrated.

This apparently—but only apparently—static attitude is to be found particularly in traditional Japanese films (the best known of these being Ozu's family chronicles). They are marked by a *med-*

itative state that lets _time_ work without precipitating new events. The very concept of time is relative—everything has _its own_ time, different phenomena are _revealed_ in their own time. It is a way of _perceiving_ rather than following an action. The development takes place in the spectator as he constantly alters and deepens his emotions and reflections about what is happening in the here and now.

Schematically, it looks like this:

Classical Drama: Each moment is a step in the linear development toward a final objective:

STARTING POINT ⟩● ⟩● ⟩● ⟩ OBJECTIVE

State-of-the-Mind Film: The moment is a center of observation that our thoughts, emotions, and associations constantly leave, encircle, return to, and penetrate:

This way of perceiving things can be said to typify an oriental lifestyle and way of thinking. It is, however, an attitude often found in certain filmmakers in the West as well. Nearly all of Antonioni's films are characterized by this "meditative" curiosity about things and their most intensive moments are when nothing is "happening" in the dramatic sense (the island sequences in _The Adventure_, the final scenes in _The Eclipse_, the park scenes in _Blow-Up_, and the scenes by the sea in _The Red Desert_). We find a similar attitude in Alain Tanner (_The Middle of the Earth, Light Years Away, In the White City_) and Werner Herzog (_Heart of Glass, Nosferatu_). This "ingression" toward things is most uncompromisingly encouraged by Tarkovsky, especially in _Stalker_ and _Nostalgia_. In _India Song_, Marguerite Duras gives a highly stylized expression of the same endeavor.

What we have called the "state-of-mind film" does not necessarily imply such radical departures from the traditional action films as those we find in the examples above. But, typically, these films concentrate more on bringing out what is happening _here and now_ than on building up expectations as to what is going to happen later. Fellini's *8 1/2* and *Juliet of the Spirits* revolve around the thoughts, dreams and fantasies of the protagonists. Cassavetes' *Faces* and *Husbands* dwell on the characters' apparently irrelevant gestures and motions until they have unwillingly revealed the truth that lies under the surface.

EPIC INVESTIGATION

Epic investigation is very close in structure to the state-of-mind film. This type of film is characterized by the fact that it starts by asking a definite question. We do not ask first of all how a situation is going to develop but rather how it is constituted and how it came to be what it is. We try to isolate an event or a fact and look at it from different angles. The resultant picture is often equivocal and unclear, and it may be the filmmaker's intention to show that truth is not constant but always depends on who sees it and from where.

For example, Orson Welles' *Citizen Kane* first shows us the documentary "official" picture of the protagonist and later—through the testimony of five different people—penetrates the façade of the myth and shows a complex person who never allows himself to be fully captured and explained. In Kurosawa's *Rashomon* four different people tell the same story (about rape and murder—or was it?) and leave the spectator with four different "truths," all of which contain both truth and lies. This type of film challenges the spectator to question the "objective" description of reality, to re-examine the evidence of the senses and apprehend what is relative in every concept of truth. The most extreme expression of this ambition is quite possibly Antonioni's *Blow-Up*, where photographic reality is itself made relative and subjective. The audience is urged to see through new eyes something that is to all appearances already known.

Epic investigation is often like systematic and painstaking detective work, which, step by step, removes layers of falsehood to find the real truth surrounding an event. This happens, for example, in Costa-Gavras' *State of Siege*, where an Aid Program worker without any apparent political affiliations turns out to be a travelling salesman in methods of torture. Another brilliant example is Thomas' *Death of a Princess*, where a cruel execution triggers a journalist's arduous voyage into the Arab world. As often happens in this kind of film, the journalist finds no definite answer to his questions but, as a result of his searching, shows a pattern of possible causes and relationships that the audience is left to ponder.

Epic investigation often ignores the chronology of events and moves freely between different planes of time. Bergman's _From the Life of the Marionettes_ is a good example of this.

MULTI-ACTION STRUCTURE

Whereas most dramatic films are constructed around a protagonist who carries the premise of the story and who also serves as a point of identification and reference for the audience, an epic story is easier to divide into sections of parallel events that sometimes touch and cross one another and at other times have their own independent development. Each chain of events has its own "protagonists," and what binds them together is the fact that each event, in its own way, illuminates the overall theme of the story. The events often have a common setting, for example a small town, which makes it easier to switch smoothly from one event to another. Perhaps the most successful film to be constructed in this way is Kurosawa's _Dodes'kaden_. Here the story is broken up into fragments from very dissimilar human lives, which together illuminate the central issue of reality versus illusion.

We find a more intellectual approach to this multi-action structure in Alain Resnais' _My Uncle From America_, which interweaves essayistic touches about the behavior of mice in a laboratory maze into the parallel human actions in order to clarify and comment on the overall theme: the irrational behavior of people.

EPISODIC/RHAPSODIC STRUCTURE

The art of making the episodic film is difficult to master. This is most easily seen in films where several directors contribute, each with his own short film story. Only rarely is the desired effect of unity obtained. Even if the starting point is the same as far as subject is concerned, each short film becomes a self-sufficient artistic expression that actually suffers from having to be integrated into one whole film together with others. One is left with the impression that they were only presented as one film so that they could be distributed in the same way as longer films.

Similar difficulties often characterize retrospective collections of excerpts from films, such as _That's Entertainment_. The best parts of, say, musicals are picked out and served up on a conveyor belt. An emcee is often used to tie up loose ends, explain situations, tell little anecdotes, and generally act as a link-man between very disparate extracts of film.

The episodic film has more chance of succeeding when one director is responsible for all the parts. Unity of style and a strong personal basic attitude make it easier to give unity of form to the Plane of Discourse. Of course, each individual episode must be subordinated to a common thematic drive that gives the impression that, although the people and the settings may change, the *subject* of the film remains the same. Perhaps the most accomplished example of this type of film in the history of the cinema is Max Ophuls' *La Ronde*; actors, settings, and situations change but each episode leads to the same bitterly ironic conclusion—the people, whether they want to or not, dance to the director's playfully cynical tune. In *The Phantom of Liberty*, Bunuel divides up the Plane of Events in a similar way into episodes that affect one another purely by chance. Yet the feel of the film is one of wholeness—each new feature is new proof of what happens when our normal conceptions of things are turned upside down. A highly sensual advocate of the episodic film was Pasolini, whose *The Decameron*, *Arabian Nights*, etc., provide a generous menu of human folly in an unbridled world of eroticism and double standards.

The episodic film is often bound together by a protagonist, who is our only fixed reference point in a seemingly chaotic mixture of settings and situations. Fellini's *The Sweet Life* and, even more, *Amarcord* provide good examples of this. The structure of these films can be called *rhapsodic*; the narrative flows and plays along through starkly contrasting situations, goes off into capricious pirouettes and spontaneous fancies. Other films, such as Jan Troell's *Here's Your Life* or Arthur Penn's *Little Big Man* organize the episodes at the crossroads of a long life story. In this case each episode often has a more or less dramatic structure.

FREE-ASSOCIATIVE STRUCTURE

We can find films that completely abandon the goal of telling a straight, linear story with a logical construction. Their structure is rather like that of free verse—sequences and pictures follow one another, bound together only by the logic of associations, memories, and dreams. We are tumbled around in time and space and only subjective thought guides the flow of pictures. In this case we can say that the form is suited to man's *inner* world, rather than the material laws of the outer world.

Obviously it is more difficult for this type of film to meet the feature film's need for minimum duration. Yet there are filmmakers who have tried—and succeeded. Tarkovsky's *Mirror* is perhaps the best example. It is impossible to relate the film in the form of a "story." Each image has a life of its own, reposing in its own poetic light. If we try to extract a coherent rationale or "story," the film slips away from us, just as poetry loses its effect when it is analyzed and dismantled. The very attempt to analyze and "understand" spoils the experience—even when the analysis is based on academically subtle interpretations of symbols, "scholarly" interpretations of myth, or psychoanalytically tinged pseudo-explanations. Tarkovsky himself has warned us of the danger of these academic parlor games. They do not lead us into the film but away from it. We unlock the film by unlocking ourselves and letting our own associations and emotions work in freedom with the film's world of images and light. It is difficult, then, to say *what* it is that makes such a film feel complete. The poetic vision gives rise to a united flow of themes, motives and expressions. If the vision is strong enough, it permeates every part of the film and pushes out anything extraneous.

We also find this associative flood of inner truth in several of Alain Resnais' films, particularly in *Last Year at Marienbad* and *I Love You, I Love You.* In *Edvard Munch*, Peter Watkins goes one step further and weaves together the subjective flow of association with external, apparently objective, observations.

Even in films that follow a chronological development of action in their overall perspective, some free association can be woven into the story. This is done, for example, with irresistible power by Dalton Trumbo in *Johnny Got His Gun.*

However, it is most common to find pure poetic form in short films. Poetry must follow its own rules and decide its own time.

16

EPIC ELEMENTS

NARRATIVE PRESENCE

The typical epic situation is one where somebody *recounts* something to somebody else. In this case, the listener or spectator has a direct and concrete experience of the *person* who tells the story. It is clear at all times that everything is seen as the narrator sees it.

The typical dramatic situation is one where the story is *acted out*. The listener/spectator then sees the story *as if* it were really happening before his very eyes.

Schematically:

Typical Dramatic Situation

| Scenic representation of reality. The action is propelled by its own inner dynamism. | → | The spectator has an apparently direct experience of the situation, without the help of an intermediary. |

Typical Epic Situation

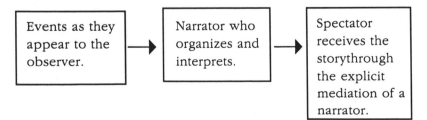

The epic film makes the spectator aware of the narrator's decisive part in telling the story. Instead of an apparently objective truth that appears as if by magic, the spectator is confronted with the world _as seen through the eyes of the narrator_, a reality that is circumscribed, defined, and interpreted.

It is quite common in epic films for the narrator to make himself known as such. Sometimes he may even _delegate_ part of his role to one of the characters in the film or program (Fellini's _And the Ship Sails On_ or Ophuls' _La Ronde_). In these cases, however, the pseudo-narrator is often _unreliable_; as an audience we should be as skeptical of him as we are of everything else. And in any case, the _real_ narrator is the one who controls the Plane of Discourse, which the pseudo-narrator does _not_ do.

Finally, we can mention those cases where the narrator (filmmaker) appears in front of the camera and acts as our guide (e.g. David Attenborough in _The Living Planet_).

Further comment on narrative presence can be found in the Point of View chapter.

METHODICAL LIMITATION OF PERSPECTIVE

Classical drama works with a _concentration_ of reality, which contains all the information that is important to the development of the action. The epic portrayal, on the other hand, sees things from a clearly delineated narrative point of view, _a vantage point that limits the information to what is available to the narrator_. Our knowledge of events is therefore reduced to the observations and interpretations which are put forward by the narrator. And he cannot give the impression of being in some sort of privileged, omniscient position; his view of the world is _relative_—he can only look at it through _his own_ eyes, from _his own_ point of view. He no longer holds the key but looks at events obliquely, from the outside, through eyes that can be either unsuspecting or critical of what he sees. Reality itself has become problematic. The question then arises, Is there any _advantage_ in this limitation of perspective implied by the epic point of view?

The restricted point of view, with its reduced access to information, is naturally inferior to the omniscient position as regards the observation and explanation of events. The question is whether the very idea of an all-knowing viewpoint is not just an attractive illusion. The seemingly objective access to all the information and all the factors that explain an event can probably never be any more than a reflection of *conventional views* as to what reality is supposed to look like, how human motivation works, how cause-and-effect relationships work. It is therefore highly doubtful whether the omniscient viewpoint is sufficient for the person who wants to *investigate* reality. His intention is to *question* our conventional views about motivation, relationships, causal connections, etc., and therefore he cannot take any truth about reality for granted.

The epic narrative approach can be an explicit reminder to the audience that each "truth" about reality depends on the perspective from which it is viewed. So the limiting of perspective is a means of defining and specifying the conditions for what we think we know. In Angelopoulos' *The Travelling Players* we follow the actors in distant shots; we never get the chance to separate them from their physical, social, and political context. But precisely this restriction of our access to individual and psychological information opens our eyes to the *historical* pattern through which the actors move. Causal connections that are easily erased in a conventional feature film become clear and lucid here for the very reason that the limiting of perspective focuses on this type of context.

It is from such a method of observation that the final scene in Antonioni's *The Passenger* gets its meaning. Here the attention of the audience is kept on what is going on *outside* the window while the protagonist is murdered (or was it murder?) in a part of the room that we cannot see. In this way we are invited to observe a series of apparently irrelevant events with a scrutiny we would not normally exercise. Is there a pattern in what we see? Does this pattern suggest a solution to the puzzle? The limited perspective forces us to activate our own ability to see.

PERSONALIZED AESTHETICS, PERSONALIZED STYLE

The Plane of Discourse in epic films has a *relatively* independent function: to clarify, interpret, and comment on what happens on the Plane of Events. While the dramatic film tries to *conceal* the devices of narrative technique, in epic films it is vital that we notice the *way* in which events and situations are rendered to us. It is through his narrative style that the filmmaker makes us aware of his presence. He acts openly as the one who shapes or interprets the fictional or factual world of the film.

When the narrative method is homogeneous and coherent, it becomes an aesthetic attitude, a *characteristic of style*. This means that we should take care not to mix narrative devices any old way we choose. Rather, we select those devices that best lend themselves to our personal view of things. A deliberate and consistent style is more than just a pretty face on things; it expresses an *attitude* toward the subject of the film. It is reality as scrutinized by *somebody*. The more anonymous and self-effacing the narrative method, the easier it is to create a false impression of objectivity. This is precisely what the epic film tries to avoid.

For example, when Antonioni has many of his scenes dominated by inanimate objects and empty spaces, this is a way of giving form to *human* relations. The spaces become psychological expanses where human emotions harden and go astray. The sense of reality called forth by these means could not come about in any other way. It is not an objective view of the world, it is Antonioni's view of the world. And that is what makes it artistically interesting.

AESTHETIC DISTANCING AND BREACH OF THE FILMIC ILLUSION—THE EFFECTS OF *VERFREMDUNG*

The strict, logical construction of a classical drama presupposes that we have access to those factors that make people act and react as they do. At the basis of this is a series of suppositions about human *motivation* and *attributes of character*. We must be able to isolate, observe, and control these building blocks or else the driving force of the drama—the chains of cause and effect in the development of the action—cannot be maintained. Thus, we can say that there is a tacit agreement behind the drama: a *view of man* and, by extension, a *way of looking at the world*.

In other words, we assume that man, the active human being, is *familiar*. Our actions are understood on the basis of a view of the world that we all tacitly share.

Drama gives this world life, succinctness, and intensity. This is its strength.

But can we blithely assume that the preconditions for action are familiar? Is there some sort of yardstick that will show us the ultimate *truth* about life? If we answer no—and only the most naive and unthinking of us dare answer in the affirmative—our common view of man and our understanding of the world is merely an expression of *convention*, an *accustomed way of seeing things*.

To the extent that classical drama has a conventional grasp of things as a precondition, it *reflects and consolidates* our accustomed view of the world. Within the framework of the drama, these conventional views cannot be questioned, since the drama's power of suggestion and illusion is based on them.

But this excludes other ways of looking at things.

One of the intentions behind many epic films is to question those conventions that lie at the root of our accustomed way of seeing things. And since the dramatic illusion of reality is built on these very conventions, the epic way of looking at things often *shatters* the effect of illusion. We are thrown out of the illusory world and perceive it as an artificial and conventional product. We are reminded that we do not necessarily have to see things in that particular way. It is just that we are *used to* seeing things in that way. But this perhaps shows us only a small part of the truth. In order to see other parts of the truth—those parts that elude or perhaps even challenge the conventional way of looking at things, we have to be able to see through and behind the illusion. We need to stand back and look at the illusion from a critical distance. We might call this technique *epic/aesthetic distancing*. The purpose of the epic distancing is to remind us of the arbitrary element in a conventional way of seeing things. It warns us against taking for granted what we are used to. We are encouraged to see things with new eyes. We are taken on a voyage of discovery, but it is a voyage whose aim is to discover new and unexpected connections.

Brecht called these distancing techniques *Verfremdung*. Things we are used to seeing from a certain point of view suddenly appear in a wholly unexpected light. The familiar appears unknown. It is as if we are seeing it for the first time. Things that we took for granted turn out to be mere convention, perhaps even fakes. Detaching ourselves—taking the step back—has made us open our eyes and allows us to see things as we have never seen them before.

The epic distancing does not, however, eliminate the power of the fictional universe. What happens is that an action is shown *at the same time as* the filmmaker takes a step back and shows us the *conditions under which we are seeing things*. The narrative *form* becomes visible. We are invited to notice *how* the filmmaker manipulates the Plain of Events. We are reminded of the fact that what is shown is only one of many possible ways of seeing it. The spectator is invited to keep at a reflective distance from the action. The detachment enables him to experience things and analyze them at the same time. The dramatic illusion is broken (to a greater or lesser extent, depending on how radical the effects of _Verfremdung_ are) but in recompense we are taken on a journey through a world which has been rendered complex and which now opens up to constantly new discoveries and insights. We are not only led into the action but _confronted_ by it, to say it as Brecht would. Where traditional drama brings about its effect of catharsis, the epic film urges us to action and insight.

Perhaps the director who worked most consistently with techniques of distancing with the aim of revealing and questioning the image of reality projected by conventional film is Jean-Luc Godard. His "film-critical" films have left their mark on filmmakers such as Woody Allen (_Annie Hall_) and Alain Tanner (_Jonas_).

ALTERNATING PLANES OF ILLUSION

One possible, though very difficult, way of enticing the spectator to keep at a reflective and activating distance is to have several different types of representation in one and the same film. For example, documentary or pseudo documentary scenes may interchange with the fictional scenes, as in Wajda's _Man of Marble_. When this succeeds, the effect is that one type of representation throws the other into critical relief. The critical element on the documentary plane makes the fictional part seem bound by convention while the fictional perspective may open our eyes to the gaps in the apparently objective documentary account of things. As an audience, we test the one against the other. We are constantly reminded of the element of _relativity_ in every method of representation. The switching between planes of illusion activates the imagination and opens up the way to an equivocal and complex reality where we do not assume in advance which perspective is right.

Example: In the last minutes of Resnais' _Providence_, a strongly subjective account (where fantasies and phobias often guide the associative flow of images) switches to a narrative form in traditional realistic style. People and relationships suddenly appear to be completely different from what they were in the high-strung subjective account. Which perspective is nearest the truth? The "objective" account cannot penetrate the surface; we have to rely on the ambiguity of the language of words, looks, gesture, and body language. On the other hand, the subjective account is formed by rationalization, projection, desires, etc. There is no unequivocal truth in either perspective. The subjective makes us examine the objective more closely, and the objective shows up the bias in the subjective.

One film maker who brilliantly lets different planes of reality intermingle is Bunuel. In his "surrealism" dreams, fantasies and phobias have the same status as what is conventionally realistic. Surfaces are broken, nothing is what it seems to be, interior and exterior reality blend together. The commonplace becomes mysterious and dangerous, what was suppressed and denied is given face and form. We *see* what is invisibly present.

NON-LINEAR TREATMENT OF TIME

When the logical, chronological order of scenes is broken, the clear cause-and-effect relationships, which we associate with dramatic narrative, become elusive. We can no longer be so sure that it was action A that *caused* action B. But perhaps the filmmaker's intention is to show us that it is not so simple. He may want to show that there are certain *patterns* in human behavior that are repeated at different times in different places, even though the events are not connected to each other. The broken, non-chronological treatment of time enables us to *see* these patterns more easily. Situations are placed side by side without having any direct dependence on each other and reveal, in this way, certain common traits that would not otherwise be so clear. Inter-connections that would be much more difficult to see in a linear sequence of scenes become apparent.

In Angelopoulos' *The Travelling Players* we are thrown back and forth between different points in time in modern Greek history. The shifts in time come suddenly and unannounced and only later do we become aware of them. This temporary confusion has a creative purpose: the political constellations are undergoing great changes and yet the changes may be just superficial. The actors have changed but the play is the same. The old regime appears in new guises. Nothing has changed basically. The disrupted chronology allows us to discover all the old things in what is apparently new.

The director who has most radically shattered linear time in his films is Alain Resnais. His abrupt switches in time show how the past is here and affects the present, although we may not be aware of it ourselves. In a linear narrative form, the problem of time could not be expressed with the same cool clarity.